The Step on the Stair

PARANORMAL HAPPENINGS IN IRELAND

SHEILA ST. CLAIR

GLENDALE

First published in Ireland by
The Glendale Press Ltd.
1 Summerhill Parade
Sandycove
Co. Dublin, Ireland

British Library Cataloguing in Publication Data

St. Clair, Sheila, *1931-*
    The step on the stair: paranormal happenings in
    Ireland.
    1. Ireland. Paranormal phenomena
    I. Title
    133'.09415

ISBN 0-907606-56-3

Cover Illustration by John Robbins; Design by David L. Murphy.
Typeset by Wendy A. Commins, The Curragh, Co. Kildare.
Make-up by Paul Bray Studio.
Printed by The Guernsey Press, Channel Islands.

The Step on the Stair

By the same author:

Folklore of the Ulster People
Psychic Phenomena in Ireland

Contents

Preface

In the past twenty years I have noticed a great change in the attitudes expressed towards investigations of the paranormal. We have moved out of the 'twilight zone' into the clearer light of more informed understanding of what paranormalists are attempting to accomplish, however inadequately.

In the pursuit of knowledge of the paranormal we are often confronted with evidence that leaves us wondering what are the questions that we should be asking. It is in pursuit of these questions that most students of the paranormal spend their time.

This book is intended to be a very small contribution to the body of evidence that can be found in Ireland. Much of the general information may serve to illustrate principles already well known and explored by investigators far more qualified than myself. I hope too that the reader will find that even the paranormal has its lighter moments!

In a way too this book is also a study of my own growth in experience and in conviction that 'there are more things in heaven and earth' than could possibly be dreamt of in our limited and faulty philosophy.

I should like to thank all those friends and colleagues who gave so generously of their time and recollections. I should also like to thank my husband, who patiently bore with chauffeuring me on innumerable research trips. This book is dedicated to him.

I should particularly like to acknowledge with gratitude the help of the following friends and colleagues: Miss Frances Hamilton, Mr Trevor Hanna, Mrs Evelyn McAuley, Mrs Sharon Anderson, Miss Kay Kennedy, Mr Bill Whitely, Messrs W. & H. Donnelly, Mrs M. Tattershall, Rosamond, Lady Langham, Mr E. Napier, Mrs U. Hughes, Mr D. Campbell, Miss H. McClane, the Misses A. and J. Thompson, Mrs M. Fitzgerald, Mrs S. Brown, Mrs V. Mahon, and Mrs M. Newby; Miss E. O'Keefe of the Society for Psychical Research; the staff of the Irish section of the Linenhall Library, Belfast; Mrs L. Craig, who so nobly typed the manuscript; the staff of the *Ulster Star*, the *Sunday News* and the *Down Recorder*; the BBC (Northern Ireland); and members of the public who contacted me with information.

Family Connections

I lay listening to that experience, which never varied. First there would be light steps on the bare wood outside my bedroom door, there would be a pause, and then the footsteps would pass on by, until somewhere in the farther recesses of the house I fancied that I heard a door close softly. After that there was nothing, only the darkness and the silence.

Upon reflection, I don't think that those nightly footsteps frightened me. I was curious, certainly, and expectant, but not afraid. I never mentioned them to anyone; it didn't seem necessary, somehow, for they were a part of the fabric of the old house in which part of my childhood was spent.

I was born west of the Tamar, in the china clay town of St Austell, Cornwall, and I came of a family of impeccable Cornish ancestry and Celtic connection; it is this I suppose that gave a certain psychic sensitivity to the women of my family.

As a child I was familiar with the myths and legends of my native duchy, and knowledgeable too about natural remedies to be found in garden and hedgerow. The respect for those country ways has stayed with me all my life.

Yet in those far-off days between the wars it would have been idle to suggest that I was aware of anything as grand as 'psychic phenomena', and the abbreviation ESP was hardly a household word. Childlike, I suppose I took much that I sensed or experienced as being 'normal'—and assumed that others, too, saw and felt the same experiences.

In any case, my psychic experiences as a child were few and far between. One of my earliest recollections is of sitting in my grandmother's garden and seeing a multicoloured flash of light and hearing a snatch of music and thinking that I saw a fairy.

Once, in the house, I passed an old man clad in old-fashioned

[9]

clothes whom I could not place among the family relatives I was accustomed to seeing in residence. But my impression of him was fleeting and only provoked a mild curiosity. Later I heard that one of my cousins had seen him too, and her reaction was far more dramatic.

When I was 7 and a bit my father moved across the Tamar to live in Devon, not far from the borders of that most mysterious wilderness, Dartmoor. I spent all my adolescence in Devon, and have little or no recollection of being confronted with any paranormal happenings. At this time my whole life was taken up with my beloved horses and shadowed by Hitler's war, into whose maelstrom one by one my older brother and sisters disappeared.

I was 18 and had the war behind me before my interest in the paranormal really asserted itself, and then only after one of the most traumatic experiences of my life.

I was looking out of the carriage window of a London-bound train, on one of my rare visits to my elder sister, when I was astonished to see the figure of my mother standing beside the railway track. She seemed so unlike her own plump and pretty self: her face was thin and strained, and I was conscious that she was trying to tell me something. How long the vision lasted I have no idea; all I knew was that my mother was going to die, and this I knew with a dreadful certainty.

Two years later, after watching her fade slowly into that thin and pain-racked image, I followed her coffin to its resting-place on a quiet Devon hill overlooking the sea. Within another two years, on board a train returning to my home in Co Antrim, I waved goodbye to my widowed father, who stood hat in hand until at last a bend in the track hid him from view. Again, in that split second of 'knowing', I was sure that I had seen him for the last time; five days later a telegram came to tell me that he was dead. That day nearly thirty years ago is as clear today as ever it was.

Perhaps what was and is important about these family events is that they proved to me that there are feelings and senses beyond the everyday, and that it is important always to bear that in mind. Indeed it was this 'family connection' with areas of the unknown that was to be a strong influence on my research in later years, and in particular my research into telepathic communication.

One particular incident stands out in my mind. On the day my mother died I was standing in Belfast beside the Assembly Building in Fisherwick Place. My mother's condition had stabilised, and I had returned to see to my own home and husband. Suddenly I *felt*—and that is the only adequate way I can describe the feeling I experienced—that my mother was dead. Inside me was such a dreadful sense of loss and loneliness that I was overwhelmed by it. 'I must go,' I said to the friend I was talking to; 'I must go—my mother has just died.' The clock above us chimed noon. Subsequently a telephone call confirmed my fears and I learned that my mother had ceased to be at three minutes to twelve o'clock.

But that was not the end of the matter. Hundreds of miles away across the water in her Essex home my elder sister was talking to her neighbour across the garden fence. She told me later what happened. 'All of a sudden I felt a great sense of cold and then an overpowering smell of hothouse blooms and damp earth. I knew Mummy was dead, and I turned to my neighbour and said, "I'm afraid I'll have to go, my mother has just died." Then the telephone rang . . .'

So it was that in a moment of intense personal trauma my mother had reached out over the miles to two of her daughters, and we, in sorrow mixed with relief that her suffering was at an end, experienced one of those rare moments of heightened consciousness that make a nonsense of physical time and distance.

Months after her death I was to feel my mother close many times, and on that last visit to my father I had woken in the early morning in her old room with the sensation of someone calling my name and of a light and playful tap on the cheek: it had been like the echo from my childhood of a gesture my mother had used when, sluggard that I was, I had been reluctant to rise from my warm bed to go to school.

Ten years were to pass before I was to sense her presence so strongly again. This time I awoke from a drug-induced sleep in a dimly lit hospital ward to see her standing at the foot of my bed. 'It's a boy,' she said with a smile; 'and he'll be all right.' Down in the intensive care unit my small son cried restlessly, for it had been a difficult and dangerous birth, and Stephen had been christened in the incubator as I lay unconscious. We were both rather poor propositions, I'm afraid. Later that night the ward sister bent over me and I opened my eyes. 'How's Stephen?' I asked. She looked surprised. 'Now how did you know you had a wee boy? You've been asleep, on and off, for twenty-four hours.' 'My mother told me,' I said sleepily. 'And she says I'm not to worry, he'll be all right.' And I fell back into a dreamless sleep.

This conversation was reported in due course to my anxious husband by a somewhat bemused ward sister. 'I thought you told me that your wife's mother was dead?' she said. My husband nodded. 'She is—but they're a very close family, and if my mother-in-law says the baby will do, he will.' And of course he did!

In fact it would seem that my mother took a close interest in the baby, for when he was 2 or thereabouts Stephen would carry on long and interesting 'conversations' with someone after he was put to bed. These conversations had intervals in them, as though someone were answering him, and even our baby-sitter commented on this. If one attempted to quiz him about the identity of his visitor he would simply say 'the lady' or 'the lady who says bye-byes'. One day his father was sorting through a pile of old photographs with Stephen 'helping' him. Suddenly Stephen grabbed a very early photograph of my mother, in which she looked young and very '1920s'. 'My lady!' he said gleefully. 'Look, Daddy, my lady!'

But while these isolated incidents over a good number of years may have been both interesting and consoling to the parties involved, they are not in any objective sense proof of anything. My only reason for putting them down is to declare the extent of my possible experience of ESP—and to point out that I never could or would describe myself as being wholly neutral in my attempt to evaluate the existence or otherwise of the paranormal event. I have never been able to see the value of preconceived opinions, and in particular if one wishes to explore the fringe areas of knowledge one may only 'travel hopefully' with an open mind. To deny flatly the existence or the probability of the existence of something simply because it doesn't conform to some finite set of rules has always seemed to me to be a fruitless kind of dogmatism.

Thirty years ago the climate of understanding was very

different from the one that prevails today. Then one found that any show of interest in the paranormal was regarded as 'quaint' by one's friends, if not downright eccentric. By others with strong dogmatic views, particularly of the religious kind, your views were regarded with more hostility: 'communion but not communication' was a phrase with which you would be chastised; and the more dogmatic your critic, the greater likelihood there was that your interest would be regarded as unhealthy, if not smacking of dealings with his Satanic majesty himself!

But even these critics were easier to deal with than the flat, uncompromising denial of the conventional scientist, and the failure to accept the possibility that there were areas of natural phenomena that could neither be weighed nor measured and whose constituents could not be duplicated in a laboratory. I suppose we all find it hard to come to terms with areas of being that do not conform with what we 'know' to be so, and life is so much easier when it is tidy and predictable; a rogue area such as the study of the paranormal must be rather disconcerting to the conventional mind.

Beyond our safe and tidy world lies a whole continent to be explored, where the barriers are gradually being pushed back and where time and space take on a new dimension, where the marvels of the human mind can only be guessed at, and there are so many infinite possibilities.

As someone who has been searching for answers over the last twenty-odd years I cannot offer any watertight explanation of the nature of the events recorded in this book. I have, however, included some suggestions and reiterated theories that might prove worth consideration—but there are as yet no definite answers. Perhaps somewhere, some day soon, a key will turn in a door and we shall have the secret revealed. I hope so.

My own journey along the road of discovery was sparked off by a prosaic request by the BBC in Northern Ireland in the early 1960s to research and write a programme on 'the supernatural'. Three months and hundreds of yards of recording tape later I was 'hooked' on the study of the paranormal, and with blissful ignorance as my only companion I set out on my own voyage of discovery. The only concrete discovery I have made in that time is that I am a devout coward. Countless journalists over the years have asked, 'But aren't you ever afraid?' I simply reply, 'Yes!', reflecting that there must be far more comfortable and less bizarre activities than 'ghost-hunting', and certainly less frustrating and time-consuming hobbies than trying to finalise and correlate witnesses' reports of events paranormal! But curiosity is a terrible affliction, and whereas I may have been 'behind the door' when the Almighty gave out courage, I was certainly in the front row when he gave out curiosity! My quest has really been no more high-minded than that.

As for the more academic questions, as to whether for example we survive bodily dissolution, my personal philosophy is that if we do then it is not a matter of belief but a matter of fact. If I am right, then non-believer and believer alike will find themselves in the same situation at the end of our finite day, whether they would or not.

Finally, it is to be hoped that some of the incidents recorded in this book may jog someone's memory, so that they too may recall some event that might help to fit another piece into the jigsaw.

Banshee

Sometimes in the pursuit of 'facts' one can be too ruthless in the rooting out of ancient custom and tradition from reports. Over thirty years I have grown to realise that much that we dismiss as 'old wives' tales' does in fact contain the essential ingredient of truth. Such is the case with that legendary messenger of death in Irish folk-tale, the *bean sí* or 'banshee', known also as the *badhbh chaointe* (crying fairy), the *bean chaointe* (crying woman), or the *beainín* (little woman). The roots of belief in her presence before a death or some great misfortune are planted deep not only in the folklore of the Irish people but of other Celtic peoples as well, while other races may know her by other names.

This is not a book on folklore; but there is perhaps an important connection to be made between the long-held belief in the banshee's existence and a facet of ESP. First one needs to determine who and what she purports to be. For some she is simply a form of ancestral ghost who warns the descendants of some ancient families that death is imminent for a member of their house.

She can of course assume different forms. T. Crofton Croker, in his *Fairy Legends and Traditions of the South of Ireland*, spoke of her as 'a tall thin woman, with uncovered head and long hair'. In the west of Ireland, however, she is variously described as 'a grey-haired woman moaning or crying' or 'a hag with elf-locks'; while in the north of Ireland she often takes the form of a beautiful young girl with red hair, who keens or laments in Irish. Most of the Ulster banshees appear to be *roe* or red-haired: there is the Maeve Roe of the Macquillans, Nein Roe of the O'Neills, and Gráinne Roe of the O'Cahans. The claim that she only attaches herself to the descendants of the ancient 'Milesian' race may be supported by the fact that

[15]

archaeologists think that red hair was common among the Goidelic or Celtic peoples who came to Ireland via Spain in early times.

Sometimes she is seen as a *beainín* or little woman: a source from Co Westmeath described her as 'a little woman about the size of a doll, with long red hair, a lovely red dress down to her toes, a red cape on her shoulders . . .'

In McAnally's *Irish Wonders* there is a report of a number of banshees manifesting simultaneously—a most unusual event. According to McAnally it happened before the death of a Galway O'Flaherty:

> Singing was suddenly heard outside the window . . . a choir of sweet voices singing some extraordinarily plaintive air, which made them turn pale, for they all felt intuitively that it was a chorus of the banshees . . .

The woman for whom they sang died a few days later.

This is not the only account of 'sweet singing' as opposed to keening: the Kinealey banshee also 'sang gloriously' before a death.

One of the better-known reports of the banshee comes from the memoirs of Lady Anne Fanshawe, who at the time of the haunting was visiting Lady Honora O'Brien, the daughter of the Fifth Earl of Thomond, near Limerick. She saw the face of a woman looking in at her bedroom window in the castle, and was struck by the extraordinary pallor of the face and the redness of the hair:

> The apparition spake aloud and in a tone I never heard, thrice 'Ahone' [*ochón*], and then with a sigh more like wind than breath, she vanished, and to me her body looked more like a thick cloud than substance . . .

The following morning her hostess, Lady Honora, told Lady Fanshawe that a cousin of hers had died in the house at two o'clock. She also told her that before a family death 'the shape of a woman appears in this window every night until they be dead.' The legend attached to this banshee seemed to come from the belief that a woman had been seduced by a lord of the castle in bygone times and that she had been murdered, and buried beneath the window.

BANSHEE

A correspondent of my own gave me a clear account of the 'wee woman' after a sighting in May 1943 near Tobermore, Co Derry. Mr W.G. described how he had gone in the company of two relatives to collect milk from the farm of a family named Martin. Returning from the farm, the three of them had seen in the lane 'a wee woman' about the size of a 10-year-old child. She was dressed in a long black dress with a maroon vertical stripe. On her head was what Mr G. said looked like 'the kind of pixie hood women wear'. To their consternation the 'wee woman' literally flew across the lane from one side to the other, and vanished. Plucking up his courage, my correspondent peeped over the hedge, but there was no-one there.

I enquired what was his own reaction to this event and he told me that his hair had stood on end! The youngest member of the party, a small cousin named John, had appeared not so much frightened as curious about the size of the woman, and kept asking, 'Why was she so small?'

On returning to his cousins' houses, Mr G. found a degree of acceptance of the incident and general agreement that it was 'the banshee', who it seemed was a fairly frequent visitor to those parts. It should be pointed out that the woman who had sold them the milk died shortly afterwards and there was also a death in Mr G.'s family.

In Scottish families the banshee becomes the *caointeach* or keener, and again she takes the form of an old woman, sometimes dressed in green and wearing a shawl or cap on her head. Here too she attaches herself to ancient families such as the Mackays, the Macmillans and the Shaws. Apart from the 'keener' there is the *bodach an dùin* or 'ghost of the hills'. This apparition haunts the Grant family. Then there is the Ghost of the Bloody Hand of the Kincardine clan, and the Airlie family, whose family seat is haunted by a ghostly drummer who beats out the death raps of members of the Ogilvie clan.

In both Ireland and Scotland the *caointeach* was identified in times past as the 'washer of the dead' (*bean ní*), for she sat by a westward-flowing stream washing the shirts of those about to die in battle, and lamenting as she did so: thus she sat before the death of the legendary hero Cú Chulain. In

Visions and Beliefs in the West of Ireland Lady Gregory describes the scene:

> Then Cuchulain went on his way, and Cathbad that followed him went with him. And presently they came to a ford, and there they saw a young girl thin and white skinned and having yellow hair, washing and ever washing, and wringing out clothing that was stained crimson red, and she was crying and keening all the time. "Little Hound", said Cathbad, "Do you see what that young girl is doing? It is your red clothes she is washing, and crying as she washes, because she knows you are going to your death against Maeve's great army . . ."

The great king Brian Bórú was also warned by a banshee before the battle of Clontarf.

Elliot O'Donnell, the well-known writer and ghost-hunter, recorded in his own book on the banshee that one of his ancestors at the Battle of the Boyne both saw and heard the banshee. He described her as a woman 'clad in some dark flowing material' and her hair 'of a marvellous golden hue—hanging loose on her shoulders', and that she was 'shaking with grief'. The noise of her moaning and wailing lasted for several seconds and culminated in 'one long protracted sob'. Those whom she wept over beside the camp fire perished in the battle next day.

In Wales the banshee is the *cyhiraeth*, a shrivelled and dreadful hag who calls the name of the person about to die, or the *gwrach y rhibyn* (hag of the dribble), a horrible and repulsive visitation who utters the most dreadful lamentation.

But banshees are just as often heard and not seen, as Elliot O'Donnell's ancestors bear witness—and there are many witnesses to her unmistakable cry. One can say 'unmistakable' because many of the witnesses I have spoken to over the years have been in no doubt about what they had heard, even those who had not heard the cry before.

In the 1960s, while making a radio programme on aspects of the paranormal called 'Walk the Earth Unseen', I had two first-hand accounts of her lament, which I have recorded in *Psychic Phenomena in Ireland*:

> It started low at first, like, then it mounted up into a crescendo; there was definitely some human element in

[18]

it . . . well, the door to the bakery where I worked was open too, and the men stopped to listen. Well, it rose as I told you to a crescendo, and you could almost make out one or two Gaelic words in it; then gradually it went away slowly. Well, we talked about it for a few minutes and at last coming on to morning, about five o'clock, one of the bread servers came in and he says to me, "I'm afraid they'll need you to take out the cart, for I just got word of the death of an aunt of mine". It was at his cart that the banshee had keened . . .

The second description came from an elderly man in Co Down.

It was a mournful sound; it would have put ye in mind of them old yard cats on the wall, but it wasn't cats, I know it meself. I thought it was a bird in torment or something . . . a mournful cry it was, and then it was going a wee bit further back and further back, until it died altogether . . .

The words 'wail', 'a lonely cry', 'a low howl rising into a shriek' occur over and over again in the reports of witnesses. Recently a Dublin housewife in a letter to me recollected the call of the banshee that she had heard in the company of her mother in the early 1950s in Cork:

We were both on the point of dropping off when suddenly we heard this wail or cry (really lonesome and very loud) which seemed to come from right over our heads on the roof. It stayed loud for a few seconds and then began to fade away, then became loud again—this continued for about half an hour or so, I am not certain, but all I remember was that I was very frightened—I knew the meaning that night of the phrase 'hair standing on end'—I had this creepy feeling . . . then my mother said quietly, "That was the banshee, say your prayers" . . . When my mother went shopping the next morning she was told that a neighbour, a Mr O'Neill had died during the night . . .

Farther afield, in the United States, an Irish-American described a wartime incident in 1946: 'A low howl it was, the noise got louder, rising and falling like an air-raid siren . . .'

A correspondent in the Larne area had a similar incident only two or three years ago when she and a companion in an old house were awakened by this terrible howling, which seemed to be in the room beside them. The two women became too terrified even to get out of bed, yet the dogs in the house were silent, and normally they would have set up quite a barrage of barking at an intruder. Again gradually the noise died away, and while the incident could not be connected to a death, the owner of the house did have a close relative ill in hospital, and she also wondered if the fact that they were contemplating a move had some connection with the keening. The banshee had been heard once before in the locality but outside the house, at the end of the large garden.

It would appear from all the reports that this ancient 'bringer of bad tidings' is still operative even in the 1980s. Perhaps the oddest feature of the reports is the fact that those who hear her said with utter conviction that they *knew* what it was.

That number must include myself. I woke from a deep sleep here in my home in Co Antrim on a night some five years ago to the sound of a terrifying low howl that rose to an absolute shriek. It was a short-lived affair, but in that time my hair literally rose on my scalp and I knew that I had heard the banshee. A few days later a young neighbour of mine was tragically killed in a car crash, her name being among those for whom the banshee calls.

The late Jean Cooper Foster once told me that when she was doing research for a book on Ulster folklore she came across an interesting variation on the banshee. In the Clogher Valley, Co Tyrone, she was told of a family banshee who was heard 'by proxy'—the neighbours over the hill heard her call. She asked the woman what did they do, and the answer was a very prosaic one: 'Why, we gets on our bicycles and goes and tells them.' Of course the banshee does not always use human form or cry; it can assume that of a bird or a butterfly, or even a tree shape, although the purist may quarrel with this. In fact one of her many titles is *badhbh chaointe*, from *badhbh*, carrion-crow, so she becomes one of the Irish 'beasts of battle', who came to cry over the dead.

BANSHEE

Two white owls haunt the Arundel family, while the *cannwyll cyrth* or 'corpse candle' of Wales is another manifestation. This takes the form of an ordinary candle with a bluish light, which vanishes and re-forms.

But for the most part it is the human shape that strikes fear into those who hear her. Lady Gregory (*Visions and Beliefs*, vol. 2) described her:

> As for the Banshee, where she stops is in the old castle of Esserkelly on the Roxborough Estate. Many a one has seen her and heard her wailing and crying, and she with a red petticoat put about her head. There was a family by the name of Fox in Moneen, and never one of that family died but she'd be heard keening them . . .

But who or what is this curious manifestation? There are one or two theories, and one is at liberty to accept the one that seems most likely. One explanation, given to me by a Co Antrim man, was this:

> The Irish, being a devout race, had appointed by Almighty God not only a personal guardian angel but an angelic guardian for the clan. As the angels of God are beyond such human feelings as joy or sorrow, they are permitted by God to share with their human 'family' those moments of great grief. This grief is expressed as a keening or lamenting in the ancient Irish tongue. Thus the banshee is the guardian of the tribe, forewarning of some tragedy yet to occur, and grieving for one of her own.

This theory deserves thoughtful consideration, but takes the banshee into the realms of the supernatural rather than the paranormal.

My own theory is somewhat different, but may be worth considering as an alternative. I would suggest that just as we inherit certain physical characteristics, such as red hair or blue eyes, so we inherit memory cells. Those of us with strong tribal lineages, riddled with intermarriage, have the banshee as part of a tribal memory. After all, the symbolism of a 'weeping woman' may well be stamped on the consciousness of Celtic peoples, among others, with their long history of war and tribal dissensions. So it may be that, while certain levels of our subconscious harbour these tribal memories, and are not of course bound by physical time limits such as operate on the level of our conscious mind, the subliminal levels throw up this hereditary pattern as a warning, in a form that is sufficiently alarming to attract our attention. Our own racial memory provides the connection, and we prepare ourselves for some crisis.

Another possibility that we cannot ignore is that the banshee is what her name implies: *bean sí*, a woman of the fairies. The fact is that there is a long and honourable tradition in Ireland and Britain, as well as elsewhere, of the fairy host, which must be treated seriously. In thirty years of listening to country people I would be the last person to assume that fairies, in whatever shape or form they come, do not exist. Their often stormy relationship with mortals, as told in countless songs and stories, has more than a ring of truth to it.

But whatever or whoever she is—status symbol, angelic messenger, or subliminal warning—she has captured the attention of countless writers and researchers over the years and made us conscious of 'the old ways' in a world grown hard and materialistic. One thing is certain: she is not contained within the Celtic countries by her attachment to her tribe or family, but has been known to follow them across the sea to other lands, as some Irish exiles could bear witness.

Lady Wilde, in her book *Ancient Legends, Mystic Charms and Superstitions of Ireland*, quotes an instance of a banshee following members of the O'Grady family to Canada: 'One morning early, about 2 a.m., a cry of great bitterness and lamentation was heard in the vicinity of their remote farmhouse, it was a sound that wakened the family to a state of sublime terror . . .' The following day the father of the family and his eldest son went out fishing on a nearby lake. By nightfall they had not returned, and at 2 a.m., exactly twenty-four hours after the cry of the banshee, the bodies of the drowned men were found. As their corpses were carried to the house the banshee cried again.

The lamenting of the 'fairy woman' is not the only form of death warning that can take place, and again many of these 'warnings' have their place in the folklore of a variety of races and cultures, while still having a valid interest for those who research the field of the paranormal.

One of the 'status symbols' to be found alongside the banshee in Irish folklore is the 'death coach', *an cóiste bodhar* or the silent coach. It varied in its appearance according to the part of the country it manifested itself in; sometimes the horses were headless, sometimes the coachman; sometimes it was an entirely black phenomenon, sometimes it had fiery streaks. Like the banshee, the headless coach or death coach could be either seen or heard.

For one Ulster family the coach was in fact its banshee, for the noise of wheels on the gravel and the jangling of bits would be heard by all, save the one for whom the coach came.

A farmer's son in Co Cork told me of an instance in the late 1950s when he was coming home late from the village. As he walked along the road he heard the sound of a horse-drawn vehicle behind him. 'It seemed strange that anyone should have a horse out so late,' he said, 'and horses anyway were not too common in the district.' As the road was quite narrow, he got up into the hedge to let it pass, but while the noise of the horses got louder he still could see nothing approaching. 'It was then I got to feel very nervous,' he went on, 'for the road was straight, and while there was no moon it was a clear summer night. Finally as I stood shaking with fright in the hedge the noise rumbled on past, and I could still see across to the other hedge.'

At this point 'discretion was the better part of valour' and he took to his heels across the field and didn't stop until he got to the door of his home. Once inside he made light of the matter to his elderly father, who was still sitting up. His father nodded his head. ''Tis the death coach,' he said in a matter-of-fact way. 'There'll be trouble for someone, I don't doubt.' The surmise was correct, it seemed, although the young man insisted to me that he thought it was 'pure coincidence': a young lad on the next farm was killed in a motorbike accident some three weeks later.

Of course it would be impossible to state dogmatically that there was a connection between the two incidents, and it would be very difficult to state what could have triggered off the death coach manifestation. Was it perhaps, like the banshee, a tribal recollection or a manifestation of the collective unconscious? Or was it simply imagination, fed by the lateness of the hour and the solitude of the country road? I simply don't know, and have merely reiterated the event as told to me. The young farmer had no other psychic experiences to relate, and in broad daylight was inclined to laugh it off—but it is worth noting that this was not the reaction of the older generation to the incident.

In 1987 a correspondent from Derry, a Miss F. H., gave me her version of the 'death coach'. Some years before, her brother and herself had been walking in the city on their way to visit a sick friend in a nursing home. It was winter, and twilight. As they passed the end of the road where they were to turn off to the nursing home they saw a black horse-drawn hearse, the horses decked in plumes and black ribbons. It passed close enough for them to see that it bore no coffin and was not going in the direction either of the livery stables or the cemetery. It made no noise, and sister and brother were both seized with a strange uneasiness. They continued on their errand; but when they reached the nursing home they were told that their friend had died a few minutes before—as Miss H. commented, 'round about the time we saw the hearse coming down the road.' Again this is not a manifestation peculiar to the Irish only: one comes across similar happenings in both Scottish and English tradition, as for example in Thomas Hardy's *Tess of the d'Urbervilles*.

There could be a quite prosaic reason for the spate of sightings of the 'headless coach' in the last century, and that is that it hid more macabre but human activity, in the shape of bodysnatching: the ruffians may have found it to their advantage to scare the local people with stories of the traditional 'death coach' or *cóiste bodhar*.

One or two other forms of warning crop up in my post with regularity. Perhaps the most common is the 'knocking' or 'rapping' before a death. Sometimes footsteps accompany the knocking or, as a variant, the doorbell is rung, or other bells in the house ring. One case reported to me by a Dublin man happened in 1955:

During the night of 8 August 1955 I was awakened by

three loud knocks. I was terrified, and have not known before or since the feeling of my hair 'standing on end'. Although frightened I went downstairs and opened the door. There was no-one there. My children and my dog were also sleeping. The next night I was awakened at exactly the same time by a knock on the front door. I felt no sensation of fear and went down to the front door to find a taxi-man waiting to take me to the hospital where my wife was a patient. She died a few hours later while I was at her bedside.

Another correspondent, a Mrs McC., told me that the night before both her husband and son were drowned she heard three raps in the house. Sometimes the rapping is heard all over the house, as though it emanated from the very walls; at other times it has a specific location: a bedside table, the front door, or the mantelpiece.

An alternative is the ringing of doorbells, as one witness, a Mrs J. C. of Belfast, described it to me. The event happened during the war, when she was living in Holywood, Co Down. She and her husband had just gone to bed.

I could hear footsteps coming up the gravel path and I was prepared for the doorbell to ring; I was half out of the bed to look out the window when the bell rang . . . but there was no-one there . . . no-one at all. Four days later my brother was killed, and it stayed in my mind because I couldn't believe that there was no-one there. We both heard the footsteps; my husband will vouch for this.

This is but one account of many that bear a remarkable similarity to one another. For example, in Co Fermanagh a solicitor and his wife were troubled by loud rapping on their front door for almost a week; it was always around 2 a.m. Then one morning that rapping became a dreadful reality when two policemen knocked them up at 2 a.m. to tell them that their only son had been killed in a road accident.

Another common form of warning is a picture falling from a wall, with no apparent physical cause. One variant of this is that the picture must shatter for the portent to be fulfilled, although the picture need not be of anything specific. This belief can be found from Cornwall to Co Down, and does appear to have some weight of fact behind it.

One good instance of this was described to me by a farmer in Co Down who said that his own elderly father became deeply troubled after a picture fell from the wall and the glass shattered. After a little while the old man rose and put on his 'good boots', and said that he was going to see his brother Willie—'for the picture was for him.' Despite protests the old man set off up the lane to his elderly brother's cottage, refusing company. It was as he expected: his brother had suddenly experienced a stroke and had just died in the arms of a neighbour. His son looked at me very thoughtfully. 'I don't pay a lot of heed to these things, but my father never did anything without a reason, and I know there was no doubt in his mind that his brother was in bother.'

One particular phenomenon I can vouch for personally. During the Second World War, I was sitting reading one afternoon in my aunt's house when I heard a crash and a breaking of glass. Going into the hall to investigate, I found that a large photograph of a relative had fallen to the ground, although the cord appeared to be intact and the hanger in place. I was about to clear up the debris when my aunt came downstairs, and the look of consternation on her face is not one I am likely to forget. 'It's a death,' she said; 'someone's going to die.' I tried with the confidence of the young to reassure her that it was all 'stuff and nonsense', but to no avail. A week later news came that a near relative had died very suddenly. Coincidence? Perhaps that is the explanation; but there may be another . . .

In the study of poltergeist phenomena we accept that the motivating energy has its origin, in all probability, in some human agency. So, is it not possible that the physical manifestations that warn of some future event may have their origin in some subliminal level of a human mind, and that someone closely connected with the forthcoming event may then generate the energy that causes the bangs, raps, or ringing, or even a picture to fall off a wall? If we take that step further, then we also know of cases where poltergeist manifestation was also accompanied by apparitions, lights, etc, and so in this context we may find an explanation for 'death coaches', banshees, and the like: that they too are manifestations generated by the unconscious level of the human mind as a means of preparing the conscious mind to face some tragic but inevitable event.

Gillhall, Co Down

Just beyond the quiet market town of Dromore, Co Down, lies the Gillhall estate, its great house now vanished after the fire of the 1970s. There are no remains to mark the spot where the house, connected with one of the strangest stories of all time, once stood.

Other paranormal events on the site were later to excite the attention of the public and media, but two centuries separate the story of the Beresford ghost and those other manifestations; and as far as I can ascertain, there is no connection between the happenings of the 1790s and those of the 1960s, save that they occurred in the same house.

The Beresford ghost is well known in the annals of Irish hauntings, and I am fortunate that I can take my telling of the tale from the papers of the Clanwilliam family, who are closely associated with Gillhall, and I place on record my thanks for that help.

The story concerns the friendship of James de la Poer, Third Earl of Tyrone, and Nicola Sophia Hamilton, daughter of Baron Hugh Hamilton of Glenawley. These two young people, according to the manuscript, were both orphaned at an early age and were subsequently put under the care of the same person, who 'educated them in the principles of Deism', that is to say, a belief in the existence of God but not in any revealed religion.

At 14 years of age the young people were put into the care of someone new, 'who used every effort to eradicate the erroneous opinions implanted in their minds'—an attempt that proved in the end only partially successful and exceedingly confusing for the two young people. Out of this confusion arose the now well-known promise they gave to one another, that whichever of them should die first would, 'if permitted, appear to the survivor and declare what religion was most approved of by the Supreme Being.'

Shortly after this, Miss Hamilton married Sir Tristram Beresford and Lord Tyrone married a Miss Rickards; the two friends continued to spend a great deal of time in one another's company, 'the families frequently visiting and spending more than a fortnight at a time in each other's houses.'

Then in October 1693 Sir Tristram and Lady Beresford were on a visit to Lady Beresford's sister at Gillhall. Lady Beresford was early in her third pregnancy, the Beresfords having two small daughters but no male heir.

She awoke one night to find Lord Tyrone standing beside her bed, while to all intents and purposes her husband lay beside her in a heavy slumber. The phantom then spoke to her, telling her that he had died the previous Tuesday, at four o'clock, and that in respect of their promise to one another he had come to fulfil his word. It was inferred in the conversation that the Supreme Being took the view that only by revealed religion might they be saved, and this information Lord Tyrone passed on to his lifelong friend.

He also told her that the child she bore would be a son, who would eventually grow up and marry his heiress. He further told her that Sir Tristram would not live long after the child's birth, and that she would marry again—'a man whose ill-treatment will render you miserable'—and that she would die in her forty-seventh year. He then caused the bed curtains to knot themselves in the iron hoop of the tester bed, and he also wrote in her pocket-book. But Lady Beresford was a woman of unusual strength of mind. 'These things I could have performed in my sleep,' she insisted; so the apparition grasped her wrist in a grip as cold as death itself.

Early next morning with the aid of a broom she replaced the curtains, and locked up her pocket-book. Her wrist she bound in a black ribbon, saying to her husband: 'Let me conjure you, Sir Tristram, never to enquire the cause of my wearing this ribbon; you will never again see me without it. If it concerned you as a husband, I would not for one moment conceal the cause; I never in my life refused your request, but for this . . .' It says much for her husband's character that he acceded to her request without further enquiry.

Shortly after this a message came from Dublin with the news of Lord Tyrone's death; and the other prophecies were to come true as well. Lady Beresford gave birth to a son, and when that son was scarcely 8 years old Sir Tristram died. Bearing in mind the rest of the prophecy, one can understand why Lady Beresford became something of a recluse. She lived, according to the manuscript, 'in great retirement', and 'visited only the family of the Clergyman of the village where she resided.' This family consisted of the clergyman, Mr Gorges, and his wife and their only son, who subsequently became an army officer. Despite a disparity in their ages, Lady Beresford married the young officer in 1704.

Alas, as Lord Tyrone had so gloomily prophesied, the young husband treated his wife with great cruelty; and although she bore him three daughters, their marriage was marred by dissension and scandal. Finally the unhappy woman left her husband.

After some time, however, and a show of penitence on the part of Lieutenant-Colonel Gorges, Lady Beresford consented to live with him again, and was soon pregnant for the fourth time. She expected to go into labour on or about her birthday, and she sent for an old friend, Lady Masserene, and some others to spend the evening with her. Mindful of the rest of the prophecy, she was exceedingly relieved to have reached this particular birthday. 'I am this day forty-eight years old,' she announced happily. Her elderly father-in-law, the clergyman, demurred. 'No, my lady, you are mistaken. Your mother and I have had many discussions concerning your age, and I have discovered that I am right. Happening to be in the parish in which you were born, I put an end to doubt by searching the register, and found you are today but forty-seven.'

Lady Beresford became pale and silent. 'You have signed my death warrant,' she said. 'I have not much longer to live. I must therefore entreat you to leave me immediately, as I have something of importance to settle before I die.'

The unhappy woman then retired to her chamber and sent for Lady Masserene and her own son, Marcus Beresford, a boy of 14, and to them she related her strange secret, which until that time she had revealed to no-one. She requested them to remove the ribbon from her wrist at her death. Shortly after this she went into labour, and within the next few hours she died. As promised, her son unbound her wrist, to reveal a scarred and shrivelled disfigurement—as the manuscript says, 'every nerve withered, every sinew shrunk'.

There are several minor variants to this classic tale. Mina Lenox-Conyngham, in *An Old Ulster House*, her book about her family home at Springhill, Co Derry, conjectures that the woman present at the deathbed was Lady Beresford's daughter, Lady Riveston, mother of Lady Betty Cobb, who was said to be in possession of the pocket-book in which the apparition had written; but the Clanwilliam papers state clearly that it was Lady Masserene. The famous 'ghost cabinet', on which the mark of a hand can be seen burned indelibly into the woodwork, is in the possession of the Clanwilliam family. I am indebted to the Rev Brett Ingram of Ballygawley for information about an alternative suggestion that gained some credence in Co Tyrone: that the apparition visited Lady Beresford not at Gillhall but at Ballygawley Castle. In *Shane Leslie's Ghost Book* the apparition is placed in Gillhall, according to information from an earlier manuscript; and while the portrait of Nicola Beresford wearing the famous black ribbon does not appear to have survived, Sir Shane did claim that he had seen the original ribbon preserved as a family keepsake. Whatever the entire truth of the matter from the point of view of geography, what is important is that the apparition would have visited Lady Beresford wherever she might have been that night. It was to her and no other that Lord Tyrone appeared, and on that one occasion only.

As a matter of interest, the final part of the prophecy came true as well, as four years after Lady Beresford's death her son Marcus married Catherine, Lord Tyrone's heiress, and so the story is completed.

It may be worth noting that the children of Marcus Beresford found fame in their own ways. One became Archbishop of Tuam and First Baron Decies; one was the Hon John Beresford, described at one time as 'virtually king of Ireland'; and the third brother became the First Marquis of Waterford. Of the Waterford Beresfords there is another tale, concerning a famous curse. It is said that the family were cursed by the mother of a man hanged for some petty crime at Seskin, Carrick-on-Suir. The curse proclaimed the death by violence of the heir to the title: 'that they would not die in their beds for seven generations.' There is stark historical proof of the efficacy of this curse.

In the 1960s Gillhall was in the news again, although in the lapse of time between the Beresford incident and the later events there are isolated reports of psychic phenomena, none of any sustained interest. One related in the late nineteenth century was that if any guests were put to sleep in the chamber over the main door they would hear in the early hours the rattle of a coach drawing up to the door. If they chanced to look out of the window they would see a young lady in a travelling-cloak alighting. Some guests reported seeing the coach run in under the *porte-cochère* long after this had been removed. The manifestation seemed to have no particular significance, and we cannot be sure that this was the chamber associated with the Beresford ghost. This room is spoken of as being 'off a gallery room on the first landing'.

Another intriguing story told to me by Lord Clanwilliam is worthy of note, and concerns the family's move from Gillhall to Montalto, Ballynahinch, Co Down.

A valuable mirror was taken down to be crated and was left in an empty room to await transport to Montalto. It was no ordinary mirror, but one that was considered 'unfortunate' for a member of the family to look into. Because of this it had been hung high up on a wall where only those of great determination or giraffe-like attributes could admire themselves. The mirror was lifted down and very carefully packed and laid on the floor, well away from other heavy furniture. The next morning, when the men came to lift the crate ominous grating sounds reached their ears, and upon investigation they found that the mirror so carefully crated now lay in a thousand pieces—'no one piece larger than my little fingernail', Lord Clanwilliam said ruefully. How such an accident took place in an empty house and to an article already crated is a matter for conjecture.

Gillhall acquired a personal significance for me in June 1961 when I was invited by a tape recording society to keep a vigil in the house. Some of the group had been visiting Gillhall to make recordings; what they heard on those tapes made them anxious to return to verify their findings, and they felt that someone with knowledge of the paranormal would be helpful, and I was happy to be of help.

The house itself was of conventional design, with three floors, a basement, and a very elegant staircase leading up to the first-floor gallery. Parts of the house had been added at a later date, but in general it was much the same as when it was built. There was a so-called 'haunted bedroom' on the second floor at the front of the house, and on the glass of the window a verse was inscribed with some sharp instrument:

> *The beauty of holiness is best understood*
> *To him that beauty beheld*
> *By the fair and the good.*

According to local legend this verse had been inscribed there by a young woman, the daughter of the house, who had involved herself in an 'unsuitable' love affair and been confined to her room by her parents. It is said that she used a diamond ring given by her beloved, and that she attempted to protest by setting fire to the bed-hangings, and was subsequently burned to death—a legend not without precedent, even if the verse is unique. Certainly the room bore evidence of a fire having ravaged it at some time, but I could find no other support for the story.

We arrived to set up our electrical monitoring system on a lovely June evening, and with expert technical assistance we turned one downstairs room into our headquarters for the night. Technicians installed microphones in the main rooms, and these were connected to a tape bank that would be monitored constantly during the night. It was decided that in the first instance we would simply 'listen to the house' by means of the equipment; then at intervals observers would walk round the house to report back any visual information. The main areas wired for sound were the hallway, the main cellar, the 'haunted room', and another large room on the upper floor. We had to supply our own generating power, and observers with walkie-talkie sets covered the grounds. To the rear of the house was a compound where the estate gun-dogs were kept, and these added to our problems during the night by howling at intervals. After a while we timed the howls, and they appeared to precede paranormal activity in the house by about twenty seconds: it was as though the unhappy dogs had psychic stop-watches!

In the previous recordings much of the activity seemed to centre in the cellars, and we paid particular attention to this. A single staircase leading down to the basement had been wired for sound; we also marked the position of certain items in the cellar, including two lengths of heavy lead piping and some large tins of paint. We satisfied ourselves that all was secure below: the windows were small and barred, and only a little of them was above ground level, and one door interconnected with all the cellars; and so with the outer door shut and sealed we could be fairly certain that there was only one way in or out.

We began monitoring at 11.28 p.m. Prevailing weather conditions were warm and windless, with no moon or stars. Outside in the vast demesne hardly a leaf stirred.

In our headquarters room we had scanty light from large portable lamps and some candles, but it was sufficient for our technicians to monitor the equipment. It was agreed that at intervals we would move about the house in pairs, ensuring that the sound engineer knew where we were and if necessary would switch off the recording equipment. Then we sat and waited.

We didn't have long to wait before we could record the first event. The doors of the control room swung back steadily, in a controlled movement, until they touched the wall. These double doors were quite heavy, and as I had previously experimented with them I knew that they would open a few inches and then stop. We shut the doors and placed a heavy bucket in front of them, and resumed our waiting. Then at 11.50 a series of events began.

First came a number of loud crashes heard from the cellar microphones; these were followed by an increase in the strange 'roaring' sound that indeed provided an *obbligato* to the entire night's proceedings. Over and over again we found that an increase in the roar, which I can only describe as a cross between the roar of flames and a beast-like noise, would invariably be followed by some distinct solo event such as thuds, the sound of heavy furniture being moved, whisperings, and once the sound of fingernails being dragged across the face of a microphone we knew to be fifteen feet up a wall.

By 1.30 a.m. the bulk of the manifestations were coming from the cellar, while the rest of the house was reasonably quiet. By now the amount and volume of the noises coming through the speakers was quite appalling, and at times we feared for the equipment, which was almost leaping about in its sockets.

At about 1.45 the first personal check was made of the locations. We had checked with our outside units on each half hour, as we were very conscious of our vulnerability to practical jokers, despite our discreet entry into the house.

When we opened the door from the control room into the hall we were still hearing bangs and crashes from one or two areas of the house. The moment we stepped into the hall, however, the noises ceased and there was a kind of watchful silence, which I find most difficult to describe.

Down in the cellar all was much as we had left it, except that the lengths of lead piping and a plank of wood had been moved towards the centre of the room; in fact they had moved a considerable distance, and this may account for the crashes we had heard from the cellar during the previous hour. The microphone was checked and appeared to be in perfect working order. Having satisfied ourselves that the check had not revealed anything more startling, we returned to the control room.

Hardly was the door closed behind us than pandemonium broke out once again, the noise again coming from the cellar. At one point we heard a cough, and then someone humming snatches of tunes. We checked the cellar stairs again, but the moment we moved out of the control room the noises ceased —and even the most clear-headed among us became aware of a feeling of being watched.

Outside there was nothing to report, with the exception of the periodic bursts of howling from the gun-dogs. Certainly they didn't add to our feeling of wellbeing, and my own personal thoughts were far from calm and content; but then I have never pretended to be anything but a coward!

One particular incident is worth noting. The heavy front door had been propped open and a stand microphone placed within a few feet of it, its cable looped over the door. It was virtually impossible for anyone to come in at the door without our being aware of the intruder by means of the microphone; and as the control room was next to the front door, any attempt to close it or to walk past the door of our room would have been difficult without one of us being aware of someone in the hall. As it was, the door was discovered to be shut but with the loop of cable, which would have caught itself in the door had it simply blown to, now looped neatly down over the back of the door. No sound of the door shutting was recorded and no-one from the house had been in the hall; neither had any of the outside group come into the house.

The door, having shut itself, now proved unwilling to open, and two burly members of our group who struggled to re-open it found the task beyond them. I went back into the hall with them and turned the knob, and the door opened easily under my hand. I must confess I enjoyed the look of amazement on their faces!

Up to this time we had not seen any manifestation in the house, but about 3 a.m. I went up the stairs to the first landing behind two other people who were systematically checking the rooms. In the landing window facing me I saw a fully lit candelabra, despite the fact that there was no such fixture above my head. As this was only seen by myself I hesitate to admit it to evidence, but it was the only thing I 'saw' in the house.

About 4 a.m. as the first streaks of dawn lit the sky the house began to quieten down, and we went outside to speak to the group who had kept vigil in the grounds. They had one sighting to report, a light hovering behind the first-floor windows, as though someone was walking slowly along carrying a lamp. The light was described as 'a soft bluish glow'. By the time we had dismantled our equipment the house was virtually still, the dawn was in the sky, and the first birds were singing.

The master tape was played back and we could of course identify such noises as creaking boards, the odd scuffle of a rat, and those odd, indefinable noises that one hears in old houses. But two repetitive noises stood out above the rest. When we were present in the cellar the emptiness and the stone flags under our feet caused a distinct distortion of sound on the microphones; yet when we were out of the cellar and the thuds and bangs were recorded on tape, there was no echo at

[36]

all: it was almost as though the cellar had been soundproofed.

The second noise, and the one that disturbed us most, was what for want of a better description we called the 'roaring'. This noise was most conspicuous just before an increase in activity in the house and often would coincide with the dogs beginning to howl. After each 'solo' manifestation the roaring would subside, only to begin again at the next event. This noise preceded the sound of footsteps on the main staircase, voices whispering, and the sound of a gong, as well as the myriad thuds and bangs that were heard. The noise itself was difficult to identify, but to me it sounded like the roar of flames and at other times a gale-force wind. At this time I was not really familiar with sound equipment and largely left this side of the investigation and analysis to the tape recordists of the society who had invited me.

Some weeks later another group spent several hours in the house, and they told me that the kind of manifestation that had been encountered that first night happened again, but was more subdued. The mysterious light that we had seen still hovered behind the windows and was seen by observers both at the front and the back of the house. Later, when the immediate publicity had died down, I returned to Gillhall with a member of the Churches Fellowship for Psychical Study, a clergyman well versed in a variety of paranormal happenings. He remarked on the sense of unease in the cellars, even in broad daylight.

Eventually Gillhall and its distinctly uneasy atmosphere faded from my mind, but intermittent reports about the house continued to come in. There was the journalist who went out with a staff photographer to do a piece on 'a haunted house'; for them the camera refused to work and slates launched themselves from the roof at their unsuspecting heads. A television crew fared no better, with equipment that remained coyly silent and unworkable and a cameraman who got hung up on the railings. My own conscience was clear in that respect, as I had warned them of the peculiar effect that Gillhall had on technical equipment, and this was further borne out by the fact that when the television crew returned to base, the camera and recording machines worked perfectly.

There was one aspect of the visit to Gillhall that I had shared with no-one, and that was a strong suspicion that somewhere occult practice had intruded upon the paranormal. I had received several anonymous phone calls that hinted delicately at the 'inadvisability' of investigating Gillhall. In the house itself I found evidence of ritual practices in some of the rooms, and the curious atmosphere in the house itself had bothered me.

For example, one would hardly have described the night in Gillhall as sleep-inducing; but at intervals during that night, when the events were at their noisiest, I had to fight an overwhelming desire to go to sleep. It was also noticeable that the number thirteen was significant. Early that night I had counted heads only to discover we were thirteen, and it was noticeable that if at any time the number within the house changed, for example when someone went outside to speak to the external group, there was a corresponding drop in activity in the house. At the time I saw no point in confiding this information to anyone else, as nerves were sufficiently stretched without the thought of 'other forces' opposing us! Later I was to meet a member of the night's group, who told me that almost everyone who had been at Gillhall that night had suffered some kind of misfortune: a car smash, a near-drowning, or a nervous collapse. He also commented on the fact that when Gillhall was discussed, within minutes a wind rose outside wherever that discussion took place, a phenomenon I had had evidence of myself.

Then there was the question of the tapes. I had only recorded a small piece myself on a rather inferior portable recorder, and had filed it with my notes. About six months later I went to look for it and couldn't find it. I rang one of the journalists who had been at Gillhall and had taped a short extract; her tape too was missing. What happened to the master tape I have no idea, but over the years I have appealed to the now disbanded tape society to contact me but with no response.

Slowly public attention died away, and then in 1969 a local newspaper, the *Sunday News*, ran a series of ghost stories, and appealed to its readers for further information. A 16-year-old girl contacted them with a story about Gillhall. She and her brother, anxious to see this notorious house for themselves, had gone up to Gillhall. The house being shut up, they at first experienced some difficulty in entering it, and attempted to see into the vestibule by peering through the letter-box on the front door. The girl described the interior, including the stairs; but when she got into the house the entire back of the door was found to be boarded up, making it impossible to see through the letter-box. Then, as they roamed the deserted house, the girl had a second experience. 'It was fat and round like a balloon,' she said, 'but as it became clearer I saw that it was a man, with short dark hair and long white shirt or night-gown, and he was rather fat.' Terrified, the girl turned, and would have jumped out of the window if she had not been prevented by her brother, who, while he saw nothing himself, was prepared to take his sister's word for it.

Barely a year after this the house burned down mysteriously one night, and what was left of the shell was blown up later to render it safe.

To the question that I have been asked many times, whether the story of Gillhall ended with the destruction of the house, I reply by telling a short anecdote.

In the summer of 1981 two journalists from a well-known English newspaper were in Ireland covering, among other things, what is euphemistically called 'the troubles'. They had heard of Gillhall and decided to have a look at the ruin and see if there was a story in it. In the first instance they called to see me for information. I told them how to find the house, and warned them that Gillhall did not view the press with any great affection, at which they smiled. An hour or so later two rather bedraggled and definitely disturbed journalists hurried in at my door. Their tale was one of considerable woe. They had found Gillhall, and having started up the long-deserted drive the car had stopped and flatly refused to start. So they had set out on foot, to be soaked by a monsoon of a thunder-storm, in the process of which one accused the other of push-ing him into a large and insalubrious mud-hole. At this point they decided that discretion was the better part of valour and ran back to the car. This time the car started without fuss, and outside the demesne they noticed that the roads were dry. As for the push that had sent one man flying, his companion hotly protested that he couldn't have done it, as he was several yards away at the time.

Gillhall, I suspect, still has a few surprises in store for the unwary visitor.

It is about a decade since I took my last look at the Gillhall estate. On impulse one summer afternoon I returned to where the great house had once stood. No vestiges of the house at all remain; only green summer meadows and grazing cattle can be seen where once there were grey stone walls and echoing rooms. It was as though the house of the Magills had never been.

On further reflection, however, I have to admit that this last statement is not entirely true.

One afternoon a year or so after the disastrous fire at Gillhall, a friend sought me out in the garden of my home. He instructed me to shut my eyes and then to hold out my hands. I did as I was bid, and something small and smooth was placed in my palm. I fingered it tentatively.

'Right, now!' said my friend. 'Without peeping, tell me where I got that.' With no hesitation I said, 'Gillhall.' My husband laughed. 'I told you Sheila would know!' he chaffed our disgruntled visitor.

A small fragment of thick green glass lay in my hand. It was ornamented with a daisy pattern: in many ways a quite unremarkable item, for the same can be seen in the inner hall doors of many nineteenth-century houses. But this fragment had come from no ordinary house, and that I knew as surely as if someone had whispered in my ear. I have it still, that last remaining token of Gillhall, Co Down.

Springhill, Co Derry

In contrast with the cold and brooding atmosphere of Gillhall, Springhill, near the small village of Moneymore, Co Derry, is a friendly, welcoming house. At the risk of sounding sentimental I must confess to having fallen irrevocably in love with this seventeenth-century family home some twenty years ago when I first laid eyes on it. It stands amid quiet green acres, and one breathes air heavy with the scent of old roses and honeysuckle, while overhead a great copper beech spreads its branches protectively over the steeply pitched roof. One gets a sense of home and history lovingly intertwined.

The National Trust has been the guardian of Springhill since 1957, and the house and grounds have been sympathetically and sensitively cared for, and it is still home to the Trust's custodian. Over the past twenty years hundreds of visitors have climbed the broad flight of steps up to the open front door and entered the pleasant, shady vestibule. To do this is to step back in time to a more gracious and leisured age.

Like many of the plantation families of Ulster, the Conynghams came from Scotland to take possession of Springhill in the reign of King James I. Being Protestant and anti-Catholic to a man, they fought for both Oliver Cromwell and King William III 'of pious and immortal memory'. With generations of military blood in their veins, they raised their own regiments and fought for their sovereign, whether amid the grey misery of the Crimea or the bloodstained mud of the Somme. The family later was to become Lenox-Conyngham, and generations of men and women bearing that name were to inhabit Springhill until 1957, when the estate passed into the care of the National Trust.

Once it was a fortified manor house, equipped to withstand assault not only from foreign enemies but from the disaffected native Irish as well. Today those fortifications of barriers and strong earthworks have largely disappeared, and only the great fortified barn remains. The white rough-cast house, with its attractive wings and broad sweep of gravel, is clearly visible to the visitor on entering the main gates. Close beside the house are the signs of the independence and self-sufficiency of other days, an alien sight in our socially dependent society: here the laundry, slaughterhouse, dairy, dovecote and stable still remain. In the walled garden the famous McCartney rose, named after Lord McCartney, envoy to the imperial court of China in the eighteenth century, still blooms, and the scent of lavender and mint, chamomile and rosemary drifts from the herb garden.

Inside, the house bears that unmistakable stamp of family occupation; well-thumbed books line the library shelves, and family photographs stand beside comfortable Victorian sofas, while from the walls the portraits of past generations look down.

It is precisely because it is a family house that the tapestry of family life woven within it shows light and dark patterning and has from time to time given expression to unusual events that for want of a better explanation we call 'paranormal'; but to generalise and call Springhill a 'haunted house', save in the widest possible interpretation of that term, would be to misinterpret the atmosphere of those quiet rooms and sunlit gardens.

It is interesting that, while Springhill has been a family home for over three hundred years, it is only since 1832 that there has been any record of hauntings in the house. If earlier generations did see or hear anything unusual, they did not record it.

The event about which most of the manifestations seem to pivot was the death in 1816 of George Lenox-Conyngham, who died by his own hand in what is known as the Blue Bedroom. The austere comment written in the family Bible by his second wife, Olivia (recorded by Mina Lenox-Conyngham in *An Old Ulster House*), is perhaps some indication of the shame and bewilderment felt by the family at such a tragic event:

George Lenox-Conyngham being in a very melancholy state of mind for many months prior, put an end to his existence by pistol shot. He lingered from the 20th

November 1816 to the 22nd, and died, thanks to the Almighty God, a truly penitent Christian. He was in the 64th year of his age. Buried at Lissan.

Olivia, who some would opine was a less than sympathetic and loving wife, followed her husband to the grave in 1832, and the first 'curious events' date from that time. The Hon Andrew Stuart, George's son-in-law, when sleeping in the Blue Bedroom would find that his clothes and other belongings moved from chair to chair during the night—an occurrence that did nothing for that gentleman's peace of mind!

Then in the 1880s a Miss Wilson, a friend of Millie, the then eldest daughter of the house, also had an unnerving experience. The two girls had been talking together in Miss Wilson's room— the Cedar Room—until quite late. This room is situated half-way up the main staircase and is now furnished as a day nursery. When Millie had gone to her own room on the upper landing her friend realised that she had left her diary behind, and not wishing to be the custodian of so private a journal she went out onto the stairs, intending to return the book to her friend. In the brilliant moonlight streaming in through the landing window Miss Wilson saw on the upper landing the apparition of a tall woman, who appeared very distressed. The apparition hurried across the landing to the door of the Blue Room and then, throwing her hands in the air as if in despair, she vanished. So too did Miss Wilson, to the relative safety of the Cedar Room and her comforting bed.

Perhaps this was the same woman who appeared to two small boys some generations later as they lay in the great four-poster in the Blue Room. They told their nurse quite matter-of-factly about 'the lady who stands at the fireplace' and with whom they seemed on conversational terms. Another child in the 1980s—a relative of one of the National Trust custodians —was to tell of a 'grey lady' who touched her on that upper landing and then vanished.

But an even more curious manifestation took place in the Blue Room in the last decade of the nineteenth century. A Miss Hamilton was visiting Springhill and had been given the Blue Room as a guest chamber. One morning she came down to breakfast a little pale and anxious-looking. On enquiry from her friend Charlotte Lenox-Conyngham, she gave the following explanation, again recorded in *An Old Ulster House*:

> I had gone to bed in the great four poster and the fire had died down and I had begun to be drowsy, when it suddenly seemed that the room was full of excited people —servants I thought—who were pushing and wrangling in whispers. I felt overcome by fear, but just then I heard a clicking sound behind me, as though a door had been opened, and then a light shone at my back, and someone seemed to come out through this light and still the commotion, so that all fear left me, and after a while I fell asleep.

Miss Hamilton commented on the fact that she had felt there was a door where there was none, but her hostess looked thoughtful. 'But there is a door,' she said, 'though quite hidden by the tester of the bed, and it has been papered over for quite a long time.' The door was opened during the residence of the last owner to live in the house, and in the powder closet was a bricked-up fireplace and window, a pair of gloves, and a small bag of bullets.

The only other phenomenon experienced in this room is the very occasional appearance to the children of the family of 'the man in the black cloak'; it is interesting to note that, while the 'grey lady' excites no feelings of apprehension, this other apparition does.

The question most likely to arise from these records of manifestation in the Blue Room is who this ghost may be, and the consensus is that the 'lady' is the apparition of Olivia Lenox-Conyngham, wife of the George Lenox-Conyngham who committed suicide in that room. Why it should be her and not the unhappy and melancholic George is an interesting point, and one for which I was given a possible explanation.

A former custodian and his wife, both of whom took a keen and informed interest in the history of the house, told me of a conversation they had had with a medical man, himself keenly interested in aspects of the paranormal. He had conjectured that when such a tragic event as a suicide takes place there are those about the victim who inevitably feel guilty at what may be their own sins of omission, and it is they and not the victim who in a psychological sense become 'haunted people'. Perhaps this is a view worthy of consideration.

Whatever Olivia Lenox-Conyngham's shortcomings as a wife may have been, contemporary records also tell of her devotion as a mother and of how she nursed her six children through that dreaded disease, smallpox. It is possible therefore that the other 'visitor' to the house, the apparition seen in the night nursery, may be Olivia.

In the early 1900s, during the stewardship of Colonel William Arbuthnot Lenox-Conyngham and his wife, Mina, the family nurse told the following story of the time when the three children of the house shared the night nursery, with herself sleeping in a bed in the corner.

One morning the nurse asked Mrs Conyngham if she had been anxious about the children the previous night, as she had seen her come into the nursery just before dawn. Mrs Conyngham held her peace but asked the nurse to explain further.

'In the small hours of the morning,' said Miss Fisher, 'I was lying awake, when the door opened and you came in and went to each bed in turn, bending over each child. Just as I was about to strike a light to see more clearly, you hurried out of the room. I could not see your face, but of course it must have been you.'

Mrs Conyngham knew that she had not been into the nursery, and indeed a few weeks later the episode was repeated. One would like to think that a mother who had nursed her own children as devotedly as Olivia had would also spare a thought for those great-great-grandchildren of hers now lying in the self-same nursery; and perhaps between the children and the 'grey lady' there existed a strong sympathetic bond.

There have been other minor incidents within the house. There are several instances of footsteps being heard, and this is a manifestation that a previous custodian, Eric Napier, and myself have both had in Springhill. In my own case I heard them on the stairs outside the Cedar Room, one sunny afternoon about eighteen years ago. I was in the Cedar Room when the door opened and something approaching a light breeze passed me, and at that same moment a heavy oak cradle beside the window began to rock. I saw nothing and heard only the sound of those light footsteps. Some workmen who were employed in repairs to the roof about twenty-two years ago had a similar experience on the stairs, and at that time the house was empty.

There has been too the occasional visitor to Springhill who has made comment on some unusual sensation they may have experienced within the house, and there are those who feel a distinct unease at entering the Blue Room, but these are few and far between. It would be idle to deny that Springhill does have a presence all its own and that there is a quality of atmosphere that is unique. On a purely personal note, there is only one place at Springhill that fills me with a sense of foreboding, and it is outside in one of the outbuildings. Here relics of cottage life are displayed, and yet I find this place cold and forbidding with an indefinable menace lurking behind the half-door. Even my husband, a most practical man, confesses to some unease in the area of this building. There are no clues, alas, to help me solve this mystery.

But enough of melancholia! Springhill in the pleasant county of Derry is a house that likes to be visited, and its memories are more happy than sad. As one wanders under the great trees and through the sunlit rooms, one can be forgiven for imagining that one hears the distant laughter of children at play, or the busy murmurs of women about the household tasks. That memory holds the door to the past, ajar.

Holiday Haunts

Holidays are something that we all look forward to, whether it's a trip to faraway and exotic climes or a restful week in a familiar location. As far as experience of the paranormal is concerned it's not uncommon for people who have never had a psychic experience in their lives to suddenly come face to face with such an event while on holiday. Perhaps the fact that they are more relaxed, more flexible in their outlook, causes them to become more perceptive of paranormal events.

Mrs H. was no exception. She had looked forward so much to her holiday and the break from routine, and the sight of her comfortable holiday home on Antrim's north coast seemed an answer to her prayers. The area is quiet, with breathtaking sea views, and the village is not far distant.

The bungalow itself was sunny and cheerful, with plenty of space for herself, her husband, their two children, and her mother-in-law, who was spending a long weekend with them. It was 'just what the doctor ordered', as Mrs H. had been quite ill and now needed rest and recuperation. She also needed a room to herself, because owing to the nature of her illness she was given to severe bouts of insomnia, which were only now yielding to treatment. After a family consultation Mrs H. was given the front bedroom, while the rest of the family distributed themselves over the other three bedrooms at the back of the bungalow.

That first night, after the unpacking was done and the supper eaten, Mrs H. retired to bed with a book and some hot milk, the rest of the family following her example shortly after. She felt relaxed and healthily tired, and hoped that the combination would see her soon 'sleeping like a baby'. Switching out the light, she settled down in the double bed with a sigh of content.

As she lay in the darkness Mrs H. felt, quite suddenly, that something very odd indeed was happening:

> I became aware that I wasn't alone any more. Someone was standing in the room; I couldn't see them, but I knew they were there. Then I felt a steady weight on the bed, and whoever it was proceeded to climb into bed over me, and onto the far side of the bed. As I lay there hardly daring to move, I felt that the other occupant now lay at right angles to me . . .

The bed had in fact its head-rail to the wall, but later examination of the wallpaper showed that there were marks on it consistent with the bed having been pushed sideways against the wall at some time.

> By now I was terrified, but I stretched out my hand and encountered an arm and hand, which I felt were those of a woman . . . then my nerve failed, I scrambled out of the bed and ran to my husband's room . . .

Her husband, Jimmy, returned with her to the now illuminated room, and neither of them could see or feel anything out of the ordinary. The room felt perfectly normal, and nothing had been disturbed. Understandably her husband was persuaded that she had had a nightmare or one of those 'borders of sleep' experiences that can be so real. So having assured her that he was only across the hall and that he would leave a light on and her door open, he went back to bed. Rather sheepishly Mrs H. followed suit; by now she had the blame firmly fixed on her late supper as the author of her 'nightmare'. She fell asleep almost at once and slept peacefully until morning, and by then her experience of the previous night did seem like a bad dream.

But on the two following nights the same sequence of events occurred. They happened only once each night, and there was no sensation of anything evil or sinister about them. Mrs H. was an intelligent and logical person, and she now realised that one nightmare was possible but that three identical ones on consecutive nights was stretching the bounds of credulity rather far. The actual phenomena varied little. She would switch out the light, and within a few minutes she would sense the 'somebody' in the room, who after an interval would climb over her and lie down at right angles to her in the bed. She now knew for certain that she was not asleep, nor was she taking any medication that would produce this sensation.

Her husband was most concerned at what he regarded as some new aspect of his wife's illness, and at this point insisted on changing rooms with her. They had agreed to say nothing to her mother-in-law or the children save that she found the bed uncomfortable, which I suppose was in its own way perfectly true! Mr H. was sure that he could convince his wife that she was dreaming. In fact the laugh was on him, for he too found himself with an invisible bed-mate, although the sensation was not as distinct; for example he could not be sure which way round the invisible occupant of the bed lay. Finally they decided to shut the room up, and with Mrs H.'s mother-in-law going home there was no need for the fourth room. There were no manifestations of any kind in the rest of the house, and to her pleasant surprise Mrs H. slept well and soundly the rest of the holiday in the back bedroom.

There was, however, a curious incident outside the bungalow in the large and secluded garden. The garden was large enough for anyone standing at the kitchen door and talking reasonably loudly not to be heard at the front garden wall, the grounds of the bungalow being quite long and narrow and facing the sea. Yet Mrs H.'s younger son, David, aged 9, heard a woman calling his name, quite distinctly, as he played at the front wall. Each time he came running in to see what his mother wanted, but she insisted that she had not called him. The boy, however, insisted that he had heard 'David! David!' called twice. This incident was repeated once in the early evening, and then no more.

Despite these events both Mr and Mrs H. insisted that the bungalow was a happy place, and while they had been alarmed by events they had not felt threatened in any way.

Mrs H. was curious about the history of the bungalow, and discreet enquiries revealed a tragic story attached to it. The young wife of a previous owner had been drowned while swimming nearby; and this young couple had had a son called David too.

'I like to think', said Mrs H. when she told me this, 'that

she was worried maybe that our David might take off on his own and come to harm, and that's why she called him.'

The only other information she had gleaned was that after the woman's death the door of that bedroom had been kept locked, and after a while the bereaved husband had gone to live elsewhere and the bungalow had been sold as a holiday home.

Mr H.'s suggestion that his wife might have had some kind of hallucinatory experience between sleeping and waking is a logical one. Indeed it could have been the beginning of an out-of-the-body experience, so that in a sense the weight of the body that Mrs H. felt was her own. Yet it is difficult to see how this could have happened so consistently over three nights. The alternative would suggest that she was picking up telepathic signals from the personality of the previous occupant, a kind of 'aetheric record', and translating that into actions. My impression of Mrs H. was of a woman who, while quiet and diffident about mentioning the experience, was also totally convinced that she had given an accurate account of what had happened in the bungalow. With the evidence of her husband one is in more of a difficulty; not that I am suggesting that his statement was other than the truth as he saw it, but he did know in detail of his wife's experience, and one cannot be sure how much that may have influenced his own experience unconsciously.

Another holiday-maker, from the last decade of the nineteenth century, had a disturbing experience after attending a dance one evening. The Rev Leslie G. Davies, Rector of Castleconnell, Co Limerick, related the following experience to a friend.

He had been holidaying with friends in a small seaside town in the north of Ireland. Returning late from a dance one evening he was accommodated on a camp-bed in a small smoking-room at the top of the first flight of stairs. The room had one door and one window, but no fireplace.

Being quite tired, Leslie Davies soon fell fast asleep, only to wake suddenly to find 'two hands pressing upon my knees and gradually passing up my body until one was on my shoulder and the other close to my chin . . .' Paralysed with fright, the young man with a supreme effort managed to force himself into movement and perform the time-honoured defence of pulling the bedclothes over his head! Gradually plucking up courage, he emerged some moments later, groped about for a candle, lit it and surveyed the room. A swift appraisal showed that nothing had changed: the door was still locked, the window open a few inches at the top.

He enlivened the family breakfast table with an account of his experience, but while the family endeavoured to make light of it he felt that they weren't being entirely frank with him.

Later in his stay Leslie Davies was to see an apparition of an elderly woman, walking about the ground floor of the house one Sunday evening when he knew himself to be the only occupant. When he had related the second experience, his friends admitted that they too had seen the apparition quite frequently, sometimes downstairs and sometimes in a bedroom on the third floor. Unfortunately no-one knew the history of the house, which was quite old. There had been vague rumours that the house had been an inn at one time and that a murder had been committed in it.

Another visitor to the north of Ireland was kept awake most of the night in a large country house where she was staying by the continual stamping of horses' hooves, interspersed with the jingle of harness, and the listener formed the impression that these horses were being walked about on paving-stones.

The next day, making a tour of inspection to see if she could locate her carriage horses, the witness found that the side of the house that contained her room was some distance from the old stables at the rear of the house. These stables contained only one old farm-horse, who was securely shut in each evening. On enquiry, the visitor received no satisfactory explanation from her hosts.

As with the Rev Davies, a subsequent event was to reveal a story. After the horses episode the witness was wakened one night by an appalling crash that echoed through the house, yet no-one else in the house stirred. The witness decided that she would make further enquiries next morning, and a servant told her that 'other persons who had occupied my room had had experiences similar to mine.' The servant knew of no direct explanation, save that a previous owner, much addicted to racing and gambling, had been shot in the house. After the second event her hosts decided to allocate her another room in the house, and she was troubled no more.

It is some years since I too had a curious experience in an old country house in Co Tyrone, where I was enjoying a quiet weekend break. During the early hours of the morning I listened sleepily to the chime of a large grandfather clock with a very sonorous 'voice'. As far as I could assess the geography of the house the sound came from the hall or possibly the landing half-way up the broad staircase. My room was in a gallery that ran round three sides of the square, and the sound seemed to come from a slightly lower level. All in all I heard the clock strike three times during the night.

In the morning on my way down to breakfast I was surprised not to pass such a clock in the hall, and enquired at the breakfast table about its location. My hostess looked somewhat confused and simply said that they had no such clock in the house. Her husband, however, a country doctor who didn't beat about the bush, simply smiled. 'You've heard our phantom clock,' he explained. 'It has been heard before. The clock, you see, stood in the hall in my grandfather's day, but when he died my grandmother moved to a smaller house and took the clock with her. When she died it was sold. You're not the only one to hear it strike in its old home, though.'

It seemed a perfectly acceptable if sad explanation. I have always held that clocks are peculiar creatures, as befits servants of Time, I suppose, and it's not unusual to hear tales of the paranormal in which clocks are involved. In this instance perhaps we can assume that the 'spirit' of the grandfather clock kept time in what it regarded as its proper place!

This is probably the appropriate place to relate also what has become known in our family as 'the Case of the Spoons'.

We had taken a large Victorian shooting-lodge for the holidays in Co Donegal, near to a beautiful and quiet shore. Here, in the company of two friends, we settled ourselves for a three-week break from routine, and far from either a telephone or a 'telly'. It was a very comfortable and pleasant house, built in a single storey with a broad veranda off which the bedrooms were arranged, while a glass door separated the kitchen area from the rest of the house, which consisted of a lounge, study, and dining-room. Off the scullery at the back of the house was

a small conservatory, while the kitchen was of farmhouse proportions, with a turf-burning range and a small servant's room
off it. The lodge itself stood in half an acre of ground, its
front facing the sea.

All went well for the first few days, the weather behaved
itself, and the house gave one a sense of affluence and wellbeing. Our landlord too had been meticulous in seeing that we
lacked for nothing. In retrospect perhaps he was overly anxious
about our welfare. We were soon to find out why!

That first Sunday I was serving lunch in the kitchen and
communicating with my friend Mary (who was in the dining-
room) by means of a very large and prestigious kitchen hatch-
cum-revolving cupboard; one loaded up on the kitchen side,
then revolved the cupboard in the hatch, and the contents
were disgorged in the dining-room. Everything was put through
the hatch, from cutlery to soup plates.

All went well until the coffee stage. 'Could I borrow your
spoon?' asked Philip, Mary's husband, reaching for my saucer.
'Use your own spoon,' I reproved him, 'there's one each!' 'Oh,
no, there's not,' said Philip; 'you women just can't count!' A
mild riot ensued after this remark, but we had to concede that
Philip was right: we were one coffee spoon short. Yet I knew
that I had counted out four of everything on the coffee tray.
It was such a trivial thing that we soon forgot about the spoon,
until we came to do the washing-up. Then, as we bore the last
of the dirty dishes to the sink, Mary counted the spoons in
the bowl: there were four. 'There you are,' she said trium-
phantly: 'there's the other spoon; it must have got stuck in
the hatch.'

Yet the incident nagged at me, and that bothered me too,
as I wasn't given to worrying over trifles in the normal course
of events. Anyway at the next meal I took no chances. I
counted all the cutlery and the crockery as I loaded the hatch.

'Hey! We're a spoon short on the table,' said Philip, who
was doing the chores. Sure enough we were, yet back in the
kitchen after the meal the spoons tallied correctly. And so it
went on: soon counting the spoons became an obsession with
all of us, but no matter how we tried, the spoon count never
tallied. I would lay out six, and within a matter of moments
in the dining-room they became five. Alternatively we would

take seven spoons out of the kitchen drawer and put eight spoons back. The knives and forks never stirred or showed any inclination to go AWOL, but the spoons . . .!

Then another small but significant manifestation began to happen. The fire-irons would transport themselves from the lounge to the dining-room in the space of time it took me to carry the bucket of turf ashes outside. The children's toys would disappear and then re-appear in the most bizarre places: in the coal scuttle, the fishing-bag, or even in a closed suitcase. We soon got tired of accusing one another of being the 'joker in the pack', and then the blame would fall inevitably on me.

'We're supposed to be on holiday,' grumbled my husband. 'Did you have to bring your work with you?' I was deeply offended that the others should assume that I had any control over the 'unseen lodger' in the house—for by now it seemed pretty obvious that this was what we possessed.

Later we were to smile at these events, and I had a more private chuckle at them than my friends will ever know. Mary, one of my oldest friends, was a very practical, down-to-earth sort of person, who up to now had regarded my interests in the paranormal as faintly bizarre. Now faced herself with the inexplicable, she became noticeably 'twitchy' and prone to leaving lights blazing all over the house, while she constantly glanced over her shoulder. Even her husband took to whistling loudly before entering the house, and to opening windows— the object of which I assume was to facilitate a fast get-away should the need arise!

To add insult to injury, once we had retired for the night the kitchen now hummed with activity. The turf range would be raked vigorously, or the crockery thumped down noisily on the shelf. But no matter how often we scrambled out of bed and threw open the kitchen door there was never anyone there, and the kitchen lay smug and silent, without a pot or pan out of place. The children did not seem one whit disturbed, while the nerves of the adults began to show distinct signs of wear and tear!

The final insult was the day 'it' borrowed my new James Bond, just when I had got to the best bit, and now I was in an agony of suspense. I had come in from the garden to fetch the book from the bedside table only to find (to use an Irishism) that 'there it was gone!' In a fury I addressed the unseen guest in rude and vociferous tones!

'I don't mind you poking about the kitchen at all hours!' I shrieked at the empty bedroom. 'I don't even much care when you pinch the spoons; but it's a rotten trick to pinch somebody's book when it's only half-read!' Thoroughly fed up, I marched into the bathroom for a towel to go for a swim, and stopped dead in my tracks. There lying coyly in the middle of the bath-rug was my book, and it had been opened at the page I had stopped reading at.

The episodes involving the spoons, however, persisted right to the end of the holiday. We also noticed that the local people, friendly and courteous though they were, could not be persuaded to come into the house, even in broad daylight. I still cherish the memory of a small boy who had trudged up from the shop with me, carrying some potatoes, who when I offered him lemonade refused to come into the kitchen but sat outside on a deck-chair and wolfed a slice of apple pie, all the while keeping a wary eye on 'the House', as he called it.

So it came, as all holidays must, to the final morning, and while we had all had a good holiday there were obviously certain reservations. Right up to the last we had been the object of certain attentions, such as young Michael's rubber duck—without which he could not be persuaded to take a bath—being hidden in his father's fishing sock!

Our landlord came to bid us goodbye, bearing as a gift a bowl of new-laid eggs. We had long decided that we would say nothing about our house guest, in the hopes that curiosity about how we had coped might evoke some response from the locals. Now the landlord eyed us a trifle anxiously, and wanted to be assured that we had had a good time and been comfortable.

'Everything was all right?' he persisted. It was a cry from the heart. Like four Chinese mandarins we nodded in unison. 'Splendid. We'll be back! Such a nice house!'

He relaxed visibly. 'Ah well, then, that's all right.' And opening the kitchen drawer in an abstracted fashion he began to count the spoons.

*

THE STEP ON THE STAIR

As a variation on the 'holiday snap', I have always collected 'holiday haunt' stories, and over the years I have been surprised at the number I have added to my collection from our annual family jaunts. Lest the reader should assume that this phenomenon is confined to holidays at home, I quote the following incident, which proves that 'holiday haunts' are international!

In 1986 I was holidaying in Bruges, that delightful Belgian city so truly nicknamed the Venice of the North. As lacemaking is an interest of mine, in Bruges I was in my element. One afternoon I strolled about the fine lace exhibition housed in the Groothuis Museum, which stands on the bank of one of the main canals. It was early afternoon, and apart from myself the only other person in the lace gallery at the time was the attendant, seated at the top of the flight of stairs that led from the lower floor.

The windows overlooking the canal were set in deep alcoves, with the showcases lining the centre of the gallery at right angles to them. As I strolled down the line of cases, out of the corner of my eye I saw a woman sitting on one of the window seats and looking out at the water below.

I was several yards farther on before the full impact of what I had seen caused me to hurriedly retrace my steps to look again at the window seat. It was empty. I glanced about me; there were no exits in this part of the gallery, and the attendant assured me that no-one had gone up or down the stairs, and that I was still the gallery's only visitor.

I tried to sort out my experience as clearly as I could. I had seen a woman in a long dark gown, with her hair caught up under a lace cap, sitting on the window seat. About her neck had been a beautiful lace collar, not unlike some on display in the gallery; she could have stepped from the frame of one of the museum's many portraits. Now all I wished was that I had looked longer and more closely at 'the lady in lace'.

Killakee House, Co Dublin

In the 1970s I was able to become involved in another interesting case of multiple phenomena on the site of a single house: Killakee Dower House, just south of Rathfarnham, Co Dublin. As in the case of Gillhall, the original mansion had fallen into ruin and finally vanished altogether, but the dower house of the Massey family remained. It had over the years housed many well-known inhabitants, including the Earl of Rosse, better known for his connection with the Dublin version of the Hell Fire Club, whose members met on the summit of Montpelier Hill behind Killakee, in the ruin that had once been a hunting-lodge for William Connolly, Speaker of the Irish House of Commons.

Constance Markievicz, the first woman to be elected to the British House of Commons in the troubled early part of this century, had also lived in the house for a time; while part of the violence that was to herald the birth of the Irish Free State was to embroil Killakee House as well. Indeed it could be said that two of the basic ingredients for the subsequent manifestations were directly linked both to the Earl of Rosse and to 'Con' Markievicz and her tenancy of the house.

In the first instance Rosse and his companions had decided to model themselves on the infamous Hell Fire Club founded in England by Sir Francis Dashwood in an age when money and viciousness often went together. The unsavoury events that took place in the so-called 'temple' above Killakee in the eighteenth century need not be examined here. It suffices to say that Rosse was a man of savage temper and bizarre tastes, and it should come as no surprise to learn that the local population believed him to be in league with Lucifer himself.

On one occasion Rosse and his friends poured spirits over a black cat and set fire to it, howling with laughter as the tormented creature fled screaming down the hill towards Killakee. Whether there is a connection between such incidents as this and the monstrous black cat that has stalked Killakee for over a century, and whose portrait used to hang in the house, is a matter for conjecture—but it does give one food for thought.

With the coming of the twentieth century and 'the troubles' that were to afflict Ireland as a new state struggled to be born, the dower house at Killakee was occupied for a time by Countess Markievicz, Constance Gore-Booth as she had been born, of whom, and her sister Eva, Ireland's great poet W.B. Yeats had written:

> *Two girls in silk kimonos, one beautiful,*
> *One a gazelle . . .*

But the time for silk kimonos had vanished, and the countess became involved in the blood and violence of the uprising in 1916. Later a gun battle between the IRA and the Black and Tans took place at Killakee, and the insurgents took shelter in the house. Two of the three men, who knew the layout of the house well, managed to escape, but the third was cornered in an upstairs room and shot down. His footsteps are said to be sometimes heard running along the gallery and into a bedroom, and at least one latter-day occupant of the house reported seeing 'a young man in a blood-stained shirt' in one of the rooms.

By the late 1960s the house had come into the possession of the O'Brien family, after a period when it had lain empty. Margaret O'Brien saw the house as an ideal venue for an arts and crafts centre, and together with her husband, a retired Garda officer, this is what they intended to do when they came to Killakee. Of course the house needed quite a bit of rehabilitation in order that the craft shops, a boutique and a studio could house the work of Dublin's up-and-coming young artists.

It was inevitable that the new owner would be aware of some of the stories about the house, and some of the workmen she employed were less than enthusiastic when confronted by a gigantic cat that roamed the shrubbery. Some observers said that it was 'the size of an Airedale dog, with gleaming eyes'. The size of the work force, according to their personal courage, rose and fell with the appearances of the animal, some of the men leaving without their wages rather than having to face 'the black beast' again. Soon the O'Briens were relying heavily on friends to help them finish the rehabilitation of Killakee; but even these were to have one or two unpleasant encounters with the ghosts of Killakee.

In one instance an artist, Tom McAssey, and one or two others were lending a hand with the painting of the main hall and ante-room. One evening as they were in the hall and McAssey himself was up a ladder they noticed that the heavy eighteenth-century front door lay open, in spite of the fact that they themselves had closed it only a short while before. Tom McAssey related how he saw in the half-light a shadowy figure on the step, and somewhat nervously he asked whoever was there to 'come in'. He was answered by a low guttural voice to the effect that he could see Tom but Tom couldn't see him, and the door must not be shut. Quite irrationally the three men became consumed with terror, and on legs that could barely hold them they fled from the hall—but not before McAssey had seen the baleful outline of a monstrous black cat. The deep impression that the cat made on McAssey is evident in the painting he created as a memorial to that evening—a painting that exercised a chilling effect on most people who saw it hanging at Killakee.

And then there was the cat's companion. Sometimes the shadowy figure of a small crippled boy was seen in the gloom of the hallway. This manifestation was reputed to be the apparition of an earlier inhabitant of the house, a boy who was both deformed and simple-minded. This unloved, pathetic creature was kept in seclusion by the family in the eighteenth century—so the legend goes—and served the purpose only of helping at some of the infamous rituals of the Hell Fire Club. When his usefulness was over, it is said, he was murdered and his body buried under the floor of the old tower at Killakee.

Mrs O'Brien showed me an iron effigy of a cat that she had found fixed to the wall of the tower and had subsequently removed and placed on her own front door. The removal of this effigy would have some occult significance, and the fact that it was made of iron is also of some interest. One can only surmise that with the removal of the effigy, which may have been used in some restraining rite in the tower, the hauntings at the front door began. One has to bear in mind that the cat and boy were never seen together, but one after the other, and that the cat did appear to favour the front door and hall for his appearances. It is not within the competence of this book to comment on witchcraft practices, but I must confess to speculating about 'familiars'; and for a lonely, crippled and tormented personality such as we may assume the boy to have been, then perhaps the ferocity and agility of the cat represented all that he might have wished to be?

I did make the suggestion that the effigy should be returned to the tower and that some means might be used to pray for the soul of the child so cruelly used. By all accounts the unhappy presence of the crippled boy did haunt the house and grounds, and the room that was pointed out to visitors as his prison did seem to have a curiously chilly air about it. Later information suggests that the skeleton of such a person was found during excavation work, and in that grave lay another effigy, of a horned and tailed demon. The remains were laid to rest with the benefit of the church, whose duty it is to pray for lost souls, and it is believed that after this, some time in 1977, the main manifestations ceased.

But Killakee had other manifestations apart from the cat and the boy. As well as a nun seen briefly in the old ballroom, there were three apparitions that appeared in the courtyard. They seem to have been seen on at least three occasions by different people, and they looked so normal that on at least two occasions they were mistaken for visitors to the crafts centre. The trio consisted of two nuns and a dark-skinned man. All three were dressed in black. Each time they appeared it was in daylight, and they walked from the direction of the main gate across the outer courtyard and into the passage that led round to the back of the house.

On two occasions they were spoken to but made no reply, and on another occasion Mrs O'Brien herself was in the boutique, which opened onto the courtyard, and saw them through the window. Thinking that they were customers she waited, but they passed down the side of the shop and into the passage, and simply vanished. We must take into consideration that this manifestation may have been an 'aetheric' record of an event that at some time in the history of the house did take place, so that what was being seen by witnesses was simply a 'replay' of such an event.

This particular visitation was not without humour, for the 'visitors' were also seen by some workmen who came to deliver carpets. On being told that they had seen some apparitions they flew into their delivery van and, with the back door swinging, accelerated away out of the gate, shedding carpets as they went!

This aspect of the Killakee hauntings was in late 1968. What was to happen later was much less amusing. In 1970 a group of people were ill-advised enough to conduct a kind of séance-cum-ouija board session in Killakee in an effort to 'lay the ghost'. The inadvisability of such foolishness needs no comment from me; but as a result of that event the disturbances at Killakee accelerated. Furniture was broken virtually into matchwood, lighting circuits were tampered with, and on several nights bells rang continuously in the house where there were no bells to ring. It was also about this time that the O'Briens' elderly relative saw the man in the blood-stained shirt in the bedroom, and the crippled boy was also seen about the house. It is no small credit to the courage of the O'Briens that they stayed put and were determined to see the matter through.

I was asked at this stage by Radio Telefís Éireann to come and participate in a short filmed programme at Killakee, such was the interest in the happenings in the house. Remnants of the broken furniture were shown both to myself and the director of the programme, and the whole story was unfolded for us. While we were there nothing untoward took place, although there were areas in the house that had that 'brooding' quality one learns after a while to recognise; but we saw no cat, no boy, and no trio of apparitions in the courtyard. Certainly the chair and other items had been destroyed very meticulously, and the portrait of the cat gave one much to think about.

The other curious phenomenon was what came to be dubbed 'the Case of the Caps'. It had begun when Mrs O'Brien had found the tops of her bottles of milk removed and had blamed it on some thirsty bird. Accordingly she had protected her milk by placing the bottles in a box with a heavy lid. Following this manoeuvre, caps began appearing all over the house; not milk-bottle caps but babies' caps, old women's caps, sun-bonnets and the like. This was a manifestation of the paranormal phenomenon known as 'apports'. They would materialise on floors, on window seats, and on hooks behind the doors. Sometimes the caps contained coins: in one a Polish coin was found, in another a French franc. I was shown several woolly caps, and the sun-bonnet with strings attached.

With such a bewildering number of phenomena it was difficult to come to any conclusions in a short time, and my feeling was that a great deal of research would need to be done on the site. The day after the film crew and I left, the poltergeist struck again. This time work in the pottery was smashed and whole areas were covered in a sticky substance, including some of the oil paintings in the house. Other canvases were torn into strips in a most methodical fashion.

In time the phenomena were less violent and the disturbances became more spasmodic. The O'Briens sought the help of the church, and accordingly a priest visited the house; then in 1977 the manifestations ceased. Six years after this Mrs O'Brien sold the house, and according to the new owners peace reigned at Killakee.

The often violent and prolonged manifesting at Killakee does provoke considerable thought. One wonders whether there are in fact more haunted people than haunted places, and if this may have been a part of the problem at Killakee, along with the excavations and general site disturbance. Then there is the occult element in the whole chapter of events. In 1970 I was told by one or two local people that they believed that the site on Montpelier Hill was still being used by a local and active coven. One man had seen them moving in procession up the hill, and others confirmed his fears. Whatever the truth is about such events exerting a baleful influence on Killakee House, the certainty is that many curious incidents did take place in Killakee and were attested to by reliable witnesses. One can only surmise that the epicentre for the storm of activity were the O'Briens themselves, and when they removed themselves from the house, peace was restored. For others, such as Tom McAssey, the events at Killakee will not be erased so easily from the memory.

KILLAKEE HOUSE, CO DUBLIN

In 1987 I was reminded of the little crippled boy of Killakee, and the paranormal events that followed his sad end, as I sat in Tempo Manor, Co Fermanagh, and listened while Rosamond, Lady Langham, told me the tale of the stable-boy of Tempo. In the sixteenth century Tempo had been in the hands of the Maguire chief, and during this time a stable-lad had been brutally done to death, some say by the Maguire himself. The body was buried beneath a flagstone at the entry to a loose-box in the stables. Nearly three hundred years later one of Lady Langham's own family, investigating the legend, had dug beneath the stone and had found the pathetic remains of the child. Being a collector and a student of natural science, her relative had brought the skull of the child indoors and housed it in the private museum along with some monkey skulls. From that moment the house experienced a degree of disturbance. Members of the family met with small but painful accidents, while the family dogs shunned the rooms and the corridor that led to the museum. Finally it was thought that the wisest course to take was to return the skull to the rest of the remains. The skeleton was then re-buried in the shrubbery at a spot known only to the family, and peace returned to Tempo Manor.

Some residual disturbances remained, however, in the vicinity of the loose-box. Lady Langham recalled that they had tried to stable calves in the box in the early days of her own residence at Tempo, and the creatures had become so crazed with fear that one of the calves had leaped through a glass window onto the cobbled yard, badly injuring itself in the process. Finally the conclusion was arrived at that the loose-box exerted some malign influence on the creatures stabled within it, and the box was used thereafter only as a store.

I could not help reflecting that a terrified boy and a simple-minded cripple had both found life in long-ago Ireland 'nasty, brutish, and short', so perhaps it is understandable that they both left their mark on those places that had housed their last mortal remains.

*

It is because the feeling engendered by both these incidents is one of horrified pity that I have to remind myself that not all tragic incidents leave such a bitter imprint on their surroundings.

In 1973 I was asked to call to a young mother who had recently lost her beloved small daughter in a road accident. I found myself talking to a quiet-spoken young woman with a pressing need to confide in someone she hoped might understand. As is so often the case in these circumstances, the bereaved person is afraid that grief may have in some way unbalanced them.

'It's my little girl's room,' she told me. 'I have left it just as it was; somehow I can't bear to give anything away, although I suppose I should.' She explained that sometimes, when she was especially low, she would go and sit in her little daughter's bedroom. 'After a while,' she explained, 'a kind of peace comes, and almost always it is accompanied by a very, very strong scent of violets. The perfume fills the whole room—and then I know that Jenny is there.'

I gently reassured her that such incidents were neither abnormal nor uncommon, but that they carried within them the seeds of comfort and healing. The young mother looked relieved, and for the first time she smiled. 'She is there, you know; and somehow that makes it all bearable.'

The Ghosts of Piper's Hill

The town of Lisburn, or Lisnagarvey as it was once called, lies about eight miles south of Belfast in Co Antrim. Through the town flows 'the linen river', the Lagan, and the bridge over that river joins Co Antrim to Co Down. The town is an ancient one, having been one of the strongholds of Hugh Neil Óg, son of Neil Óg O'Neil, one of the princes of Tirowen.

Like most towns, Lisburn grew from a small village—its original name Lios na gCearrbhach, 'fort of the gamblers'—into a flourishing town, with properly laid out streets, fine houses and shops. By the seventeenth century it possessed both a castle, built by Lord Conway in 1629, and a cathedral church for the diocese of Down and Connor.

Like most substantial towns in Ulster it saw battle, plague and fire. In 1641 Lisburn was besieged by insurgents under the command of Phelim O'Neil and Con Magenis. In one assault over five hundred men were slain in the central streets of the town. An account of this blood-stained episode is to be found in the records of the cathedral, as described by Greene in his *Concise History of Lisburn*, and the writer concludes:

> Their [the insurgents'] two Generals quit their station . . . and in their retreat fired Brookhill House and the Lord Conway Library in it . . . They were so enraged at this defeat that they murdered many hundreds of Protestants whom they had kept prisoner in the Counties Armagh and Tyrone . . .

It was after this battle that Piper's Hill, a steep and narrow street running from Market Square in the top part of the town to Smithfield in the lower end, received its name, when a piper with one of the regiments had his head taken off by a cannon ball, and the head was said to have rolled down the hill. Later the hill was to house the cottages of the Huguenot weavers who had fled from France after the revocation of the Edict of Nantes. They settled beside the Lagan, bringing their skills with them, and soon Lisburn was to become renowned as one of Ireland's principal linen towns.

But to return to Piper's Hill. I first saw it in 1958 when I went in the company of J.H. Brennan—'Herbie' to his friends—who was at that time the editor of the local paper, the *Ulster Star*. Herbie now is better known for his books on occult philosophy and history.

The paper had decided to investigate the complaints of one of the residents of the Hill, Hugh Cunningham, who, as the tenant of number 11, had an unusual tale to tell about the cottage that stood next to his. 'Something or someone tramps up and down the stairs at all hours,' he explained. 'The noise is quite loud and almost always late at night—it's like someone in big heavy boots.' Now for anyone who has ever suffered from noisy neighbours there may not be anything too remarkable in Hugh's complaint—save that in his case the cottage next door was devoid of inhabitants, and boarded up!

His main grievance lay not so much in the disturbance but in the fact that no-one appeared to appreciate his discomfiture, and certainly no-one was prepared to offer him any financial compensation with regard to rent or rates. The cottage next door, number 13, had lain empty for some time and the doors and windows had been secured against vandals. It was pointed out, however, that the family that had occupied the cottage had left in something of a hurry.

Patient questioning of Mr Cunningham revealed no particular pattern to the noises, and he had not seen anything unusual. Looking at the dilapidated state of the cottage next door and the fact that the whole area was scheduled for redevelopment one had to consider that the noises might have had a perfectly common explanation in the movements of vermin. There was one unusual feature about the Piper's Hill cottages, however: the cottages all backed onto the Hill, and had no rear doors.

The ground floor of each cottage consisted of a kitchen and a scullery that led off it, and the only entry or exit was the door at the front. Below were the original cellars where the Huguenot weavers had once set up their looms, now for the most part no longer in use. Upstairs were two rooms, reached by stairs that led out of the lower room. The walls between were of reasonable thickness, but it would be possible to have heard noises from the next-door cottage, especially as the stairs ran along the adjoining wall.

Having reassured the old man that we would look into the matter of the 'boots' that troubled him so much, Herbie and I set out to find the last occupant of number 13. We finally ran her to ground in the Smithfield area of the town, and her story was coherent if a little disturbing; indeed as she told it she kept glancing nervously over her shoulder as though we were not alone. Mrs McKeague (that is not her real name) extracted a promise that we would respect her anonymity before she would explain 'the trouble', as she euphemistically described it, that had finally driven her and her family from their home.

It had started some months earlier, in the spring of 1958. At first the day had seemed much like any other: the children had gone off to school, and she had begun to prepare the dinner at the fire in the kitchen. It was a little before noon when, as she peeled the potatoes and dropped them into the pot, Mrs McKeague thought she heard someone moving upstairs. Although she hadn't left the kitchen to go into the scullery, and so no-one could have come in at the door and gone upstairs without her having seen them, Mrs McKeague went to the bottom of the stairs and called out, 'Who's there?' Receiving no reply and hearing nothing more, she returned to her place at the fire. It was now a few minutes after noon, when again she heard sounds overhead. 'It was a heavy foot and a light foot, and the boards creaked as they trod back and forth . . .' By now thoroughly alarmed, and a little angry, Mrs McKeague went to the foot of the stairs again. Immediately she set foot on the stairs the 'footsteps' ceased, only to begin again as she retreated to the fire. Some ten minutes had now elapsed since the first noises had been heard, and now, much to her relief, a neighbour came to the half-door. Seeing how upset Mrs McKeague was, the other woman came into the kitchen, and within minutes she too heard the footsteps. Plucking up their courage both women made a rush for the stairs, but once again the noises stopped.

After a whispered consultation the neighbour went for the priest, and returning with him in a few minutes both she and Mrs McKeague told him what had happened, and asked him to listen. The upstairs rooms once again fell silent, although the priest mounted the staircase and examined both of them, interconnected as they were. Once he returned to the kitchen the noises began again. No doubt in an attempt to allay the fears of the women, he suggested that the noise might be due to rats. It was a reasonable suggestion, bearing in mind the state of the cottages; but although she was a very frightened woman, Mrs McKeague's dry Ulster wit shone through. 'If that's rats, Father, then it's the first time I heard tell of them wearing boots!'

The initial disturbance lasted from a few minutes before noon to about 12.50 p.m. Then it ceased abruptly. If, however, the unfortunate McKeague family thought that would be the end of the matter, they were to be sadly disillusioned. The footsteps continued to be heard by every member of the family, six in all, and always they were overhead in the larger of the two rooms.

There were other manifestations too. Members of the family were hurled bodily out of bed, a heavy dressing-table mirror was smashed and the glass in an upstairs window broken; and most depressing of all was the cold and threatening atmosphere that pervaded the house. 'You could almost smell the fear,' said Mrs McKeague. Finally and understandably the family refused to go upstairs at all, and even attempts by the clergy to bless the house proved unavailing. The parish priest set about trying to get the family rehoused, no easy task in a borough already short of houses. Most heartening of all for the family, a friendly conspiracy grew up between friends, clergy and police to see that they were never alone, for by now the McKeagues ate and slept in the kitchen, with the lights on and the half-door open, no matter what the weather. The disturbances became intermittent, but it was with great relief that the family were at last rehoused; and poor Mrs McKeague, having borne so much with great fortitude, succumbed to a nervous collapse, which could hardly be wondered at.

I asked what had happened after the family had left the house, and Mrs McKeague was able to tell us that right up to the time they left it the disturbances had continued, and then the cottage had been boarded up. Her reply, combined with Mr Cunningham's assertions, meant that the footsteps had continued to be heard next door even when the cottage lay empty, the main difference being the contention by Hugh Cunningham that he heard the feet *on* the stairs, while Mrs McKeague had only heard them up in the bedroom.

I then asked her what she thought the manifestations were, and Mrs McKeague was in no doubt. 'It was the noon-day Devil, like it tells us about in the Bible,' she said.

The unfortunate experiences of the occupants of number 13 were not without precedent. Outside on Piper's Hill itself several curious incidents had taken place at irregular intervals. Opposite the cottages at that time were several small shops, including a butcher's and a shoemaker's. Several witnesses who lived or worked on the Hill had told of hearing a noise, 'like chains being dragged along the ground and up the Hill'; one or two said that the noise stopped near the door of number 13. This phenomenon almost always occurred in broad daylight. Another noise that was heard regularly was the sound of a woman running down the Hill, and this occurred about nine o'clock in the evening. This manifestation did not appear to have any connection with any of the other disturbances. Most people knew the story of the piper of Piper's Hill, and yet it was hard to see how the paranormal happenings, if that is what they were, could have any direct connection with that gruesome piece of military history.

There was a further curious and comical incident that came to light as over the next week or two I made enquiries and recordings for a BBC radio programme. My producer and I had tried in vain to get permission to record inside number 13, but the owner, conscious of all the publicity and of the safety factors, declined to allow us. So we had to content ourselves with interviewing Hugh Cunningham and his next-door neighbour, an elderly woman with a forthright and voluble line of conversation. On hearing of Hugh Cunningham's complaints she vouchsafed that it was 'a terrible lot of nonsense' and that she had lived on Piper's Hill all her married life and 'never heard tell of footsteps or anything the like of that!' She obviously considered us as having 'a screw loose' too as we attempted to encourage her to recollect any useful information—with scant success—and our spirits sank. Finally, as there appeared to be no point in continuing the conversation we thanked her for her time and turned to go. But the old woman was determined to have the last word, and what she said stopped us in our tracks.

'Footsteps and rubbish like that,' she muttered—'Hughie would have something to talk on if he had seen the woman who stands in my kitchen!' Hardly able to credit my ears, and miserably conscious that my tape recorder was now disconnected, I resorted to low cunning. 'A woman in the kitchen—how interesting! I suppose you would need someone to help about the place.' She snorted indignantly. 'Woman, dear, I don't need help! No, missus, this woman comes all on her lone and stands fornenst [beside] the fire in the evening time, and then she goes out the back and I don't see her again.' She hastened to assure me that the woman never bothered her, and that she 'took no account' of her nightly visitor.

Having dropped her bombshell, our belligerent informant then returned to the attack on her unfortunate neighbour, and also rounded on us. She reminded us that she didn't believe 'in ghosts or the like', and she'd no idea who the woman was, for 'she minds her own business and I mind mine.'

We did manage to get a brief description though of 'the woman in the kitchen'. She wore a long apron and cap and some kind of a grey dress. Herbie and I concluded that this might be a generalised description of the dress of an eighteenth-century weaver, such as might have occupied the cottage in earlier times. The fact that she disappeared into the scullery, which had no back door, lent some substance to this idea, as the trapdoor into the cellar that had once housed the loom was in the scullery floor.

Having recovered from the shock of this gratuitous information, Herbie Brennan and I took stock of what we knew of Piper's Hill and its ghosts. The manifestation in number 13 was auditory and poltergeistic in content, with drops in temperature, but no apparition was seen. There were young children in the McKeague family, and the entity was not amenable to the ministrations of the church. There were, as far as we knew, no earlier disturbances in the house: they had begun with the occupancy of the McKeague family. The phenomena of the chains and the sound of a woman running on the Hill were rather different. These incidents didn't appear to be connected with the cottage and were not connected with each other. It is possible that these were aetheric records and were in fact ordinary sounds from the past, captured in time.

To revert for a moment to the footsteps in number 13, one had also to bear in mind that had the manifestation been connected simply with the McKeague family, then once they had left the house the noises should have subsided. Hugh Cunningham, however, heard them for a good six months after the cottage was shut up, unless of course it was only rats.

Two years or so after the publicity had died down with regard to the incidents on Piper's Hill, another possibility did occur to me, but I had no way of proving my theory concerning the 'dragging chains' on the Hill. After the bloody events not only of 1641 but of the 1798 rebellion too, much summary justice was meted out in Lisburn to the insurgents. Public hangings were common. We know for a fact that the United Irishman Henry Munroe, whose home was in Market Street, Lisburn, and who was called upon to lead the insurgents at the Battle of Ballynahinch on 13 July 1798, was hanged in Market Square after his betrayal and capture. His body was decapitated and the head displayed on a pike. Three other men were hanged from a lamp-post at the corner of Castle Street, such was the shortage of conventional gallows.

If these events are part of Lisburn's history, then would it be a feasible suggestion that other condemned felons may have made their way, in chains, up Piper's Hill to have similar rough justice meted out to them? This possibility might explain why the chains were only heard going *up* the Hill: for obvious reasons none of those men would be heard coming down the Hill again. It is not a theory I can prove from the siting of a gallows in or near Piper's Hill, but the lane did lead to the high part of the town and to the square. It is at least an interesting speculation.

In a town as old as Lisburn it would be surprising if there had been no history of 'curious incidents' of one kind or another, and the Piper's Hill disturbances simply attracted more attention than some others. Mysterious footsteps were said to have been heard in one of the houses in Market Square itself; at one time it had been occupied by a local newspaper office, and I can recollect a journalist friend telling me that once or twice when he had been working late in his office on the first floor he had heard footsteps coming upstairs, only to find that he was alone in the building. But, as he said, 'old houses can play funny tricks on you,' and I agreed.

There were some incidents with more substance. One road in particular yielded two separate incidents in the last twelve years. Causeway End Road lies on the west side of the town. Once it had been a quiet country road beyond the town limits, with one or two cottages and the occasional farm building. With the increasing demand of a growing population in recent years, Lisburn has grown in a fashion that those early inhabitants of Lios na gCearrbhach could scarcely have credited. Causeway End Road has become integrated into the town, with pretty bungalows where once there were only meadows, and it is possible that the road may have seen more depressing sights than merely the cattle going home at evening time.

Both during and after the famines that racked Ireland in the eighteenth and nineteenth centuries, hunger had a companion, the dreaded cholera, and as many died from that as from the ravages of starvation. Co Antrim was no exception to these twin disasters, and Lisburn itself knew full well the terrible price to be paid by the weakest and most vulnerable. To be able to bury the dead quickly and safely away from the centres of population was an urgent necessity in those terrible times, and if one bears this in mind then one can examine an incident that happened at Causeway End with a little hindsight.

One evening I received a telephone call from a young woman who explained that she and her husband and baby had moved into a bungalow on the Causeway End Road, and that she felt it would relieve her mind a little if I could find the time to call to her. She seemed anxious and upset. Later the next day I called at her attractive and pleasant home, to be told a tale that was neither of those things.

She said that she had been standing one morning in the kitchen, the windows of which looked out both on the back garden and the side of the bungalow. The garden was large and bounded by a natural hedge, beyond which was an expanse of open fields. As she had been performing routine tasks she saw come past the wide window a horse and cart, the driver of which was shrouded in sacking or a dark cloak. The cart too contained objects wrapped in sacking, which for some reason filled her with unreasonable terror.

The cart passed slowly down the side of the bungalow, making no noise, and vanished before it came into view in the rear windows of the kitchen. The young woman rushed into the back garden but there was nothing or no-one there. This experience was repeated on another occasion, and again she felt both terror and revulsion. She also experienced what she described as 'a cold, deep discomfort, almost a grief', when she stood down at the bottom of the garden by the hedge that bounded the property.

She felt the need to confide her experience to someone, and also to be reassured that she wasn't going off her head. I did my best to allay her fears in that respect, while having to admit that I had little or no knowledge of the Causeway Road area. Her impressions however were vital. 'So what did you feel was in the cart?' I asked. 'Bodies,' she said with no hesitation. 'Dead bodies wrapped in that ghastly sacking. That cart—it was horrible.'

I knew of the reputed location of one cholera pit in Lisburn, but had to confess my ignorance of any others, but the thought was bound to cross my mind. Was it possible that she had seen a 'dead cart' bringing the bodies of the plague victims to some mass grave beyond the town limits? Subsequent enquiries yielded no further clues about any mass burial in the area, but one also has to take into account that some bodies were buried secretly by grieving relatives, repelled by the idea of mass burial. The only other impression the young housewife received from the area of the hedge was that there was a child or children involved in her waking nightmare.

The other incident connected with Causeway End Road was very recent. About three years ago a friend who had been lunching with colleagues in the Down Royal Inn, which stands parallel to and below the level of the Causeway End Road, was stopped by one of the company, who asked him if he smelt anything strange or heard cattle bellowing. When he replied in the negative his friend, who was standing beside him in the car park on this early summer evening, confessed to hearing 'beasts stamping about and lowing, and the smell—like a butcher's shop.'

The two men were standing directly below the Causeway End Road and a ruined stone building that fronted onto that road. My friend said that his informant was baffled when he found that the noises he had heard were not being heard by anyone else, and he insisted that they had come from the direction of the stone building. Later, so my friend said, he repeated the assertion to a local man who had some knowledge of the area and was told that some forty or so years earlier a small slaughterhouse had stood on that road, and in all probability the ruin was all that was left of that place. Again one is faced with the possibility that one person 'tuned in' to an echo from the past.

On the far side of the Ballinderry Road and only a stone's throw from the Down Royal Inn is a small bungalow development. The dwellings were built some twenty years ago and in those days they overlooked farmland. One of the fields adjoining the estate had a large oak tree at the gate, where local tradition had it that a man had once hanged himself, and his ghost was said to haunt the area. Notwithstanding this grim tale, the local youngsters used the field for football and other pursuits.

It happened that this particular development had also had some history of footsteps being heard walking round the new sites, and an elderly Lisburn resident once told me that she was most surprised that any houses had been built in that area, 'because that is fairy ground'. The fairies, however, must have liked the company they were keeping, because the whole site seemed attractive and friendly. There had been only one paranormal happening, and that occurred in the field of the oak tree.

One of the residents of the bungalows, a Mrs Mahon, had only been in her new home a year or so when one afternoon as she was entertaining two friends to tea she saw crossing the field a woman carrying what appeared to be a very heavy bucket. She was dressed in a print apron and gown, and Mrs Mahon could see her plainly over the boundary hedge. Her friend, a Mrs B., also saw the figure, but the other friend saw nothing. When the woman was about half way across the field and heading in the general direction of the farm, she simply evaporated into thin air. Mrs Mahon explained to me within the hour what she had seen, and she said that she must have been watching the woman for some time without realising that there was something odd about her. 'It was the long frock and apron,' she said. 'It sounds silly, but I simply didn't take the implication in, I was so interested in the conversation. When I did and drew my friends' attention to it, within minutes the figure was gone.' She never saw the apparition again, and as far as I know neither did anyone else. That field is now full of pleasant modern bungalows, and the farm woman with her bucket is gone for ever.

In fact the Ballinderry Road and Piper's Hill have that much in common today. The Hill is devoid of cottages, and where number 13 once stood is an elegant Italian restaurant, while boutiques and fashionable shops line the rest of the narrow street, and behind them is the very modern health centre. One might surmise that in such a modern and clinical atmosphere, whatever ghosts there may have been there in the past are well and truly laid. Yet Piper's Hill was to produce one more event, a curious sequel to the earlier happenings.

In the winter of 1977 I received a telephone call from a Mrs White, who, to put it mildly, was upset. She had been walking up Piper's Hill in the late evening a day or two before to meet her husband in Market Square. Half way up the Hill she was overcome by such a feeling of terror that she could scarcely control her legs and make it to the top. 'It was nothing I could see or hear,' she explained, 'but there was a dreadful sense, almost a smell of death and decay, and this overpowering sense of evil.' Her husband found her in a state of near-collapse at the top of Piper's Hill, and fearing that she had had a seizure of some kind, he called a doctor to the house.

Mrs White asked me to visit her at home, and I found her both a cheerful and a sensible person with a strong Christian belief. She had given the matter much thought but could not explain her experience in so-called rational terms. On reflection she likened it to walking into some nauseous gas, although she could not see in the darkness a vapour of any kind. Even in the daylight and in the comfort of her own home it was obvious that the experience had left its mark.

I asked if she could locate the spot where she thought she began to have the experience: it was within a yard or two of where number 13 Piper's Hill had once stood.

The Irish Poltergeist

In July 1910 a curious case of disturbances in Enniscorthy, Co Wexford, was brought to the attention of Sir William Barrett FRS, a member of the Society for Psychical Research, by a journalist on the *Enniscorthy Guardian*, Nicholas Murphy.

The family at the centre of the disturbances were called Redmond, and lived in Court Street, Enniscorthy. Their house was spacious and well cared for, consisting of a shop and a kitchen on the ground floor, and above this three bedrooms leading off a landing. Mr and Mrs Redmond slept in the front room; the rear bedroom was occupied by two young men who lodged with them, John Randall and George Sinott, both carpenters by trade; and the third room was occupied by the servant, Bridget Thorpe. It was in the rear bedroom occupied by Randall and Sinott that the manifestations mostly occurred.

Murphy, who had heard reports and rumours of the 'haunted house' in Court Street, obtained permission from the Redmonds to spend the night in the haunted room, together with another witness, Owen Devereux of Enniscorthy. Together they inspected the upper floor, paying particular attention to the rear bedroom, where they pulled out the beds from the walls, rapping floors and windows as they went and examining the fireplace carefully. At this time the Redmonds' house was nearly new. The four men then retired to the room for the night, the two lodgers going to bed and Murphy and Devereux making themselves comfortable in two chairs. It was about 11.20 p.m. when the lamp was extinguished. In order to facilitate the witnesses, however, the window blind was left up and the curtains pulled back, so it was possible to distinguish quite well the outlines of furniture and the contours of the room.

About ten minutes after 'lights out' a tapping noise was

heard close to the foot of John Randall's bed. The taps started slowly, and Devereux remarked that it sounded like 'a rat eating at timber'. George Sinott replied, 'You'll soon see the rat it is.' The tapping rate increased gradually until it reached approximately 100 to 120 raps a minute. As it grew faster so it grew louder, lasting about five minutes and then ceasing abruptly. Almost at once John Randall complained that his bedclothes were sliding off the bed. A match was struck and it was noticed that the clothes had been drawn in a diagonal fashion towards the foot of the bed, while the overhang seemed to be drawn under the bed as though the bedclothes were in a strong draught. There was no other disturbance in the room. The two witnesses searched underneath the bed but could find no sign of trickery, and so the light was once more extinguished. After ten minutes or so the rapping began again, and speeded up and then ceased as abruptly as before. Then the pulling at the bedclothes repeated itself, with Randall shouting out, 'I can't hold them! They are going—and I am going with them! There is something pushing me . . . !' And with that, Randall was deposited on the floor with all the bedclothes, including the bottom sheet. The unfortunate man was bathed in perspiration and trembling all over. His companion, in bed on the far side of the room, shot up in his bed and seemed exceedingly frightened. According to Murphy's meticulous account, neither man appeared to be feigning terror: both were genuinely scared out of their wits.

Despite this, Murphy managed to persuade John Randall to get back into bed and re-adjust the bedclothes, the time now being shortly before midnight. Redmond, Murphy and Devereux continued to monitor the situation, and at about five minutes past midnight the rapping started again but in a different location, a spot half way between the two beds. The noise continued for some fifteen minutes, then it ceased. At 3 a.m., as nothing further had happened, Murphy and Devereux left the house, and Redmond returned to his own room. Both Murphy and Devereux returned the next night, while Randall and Sinott were away visiting their families, and on that occasion nothing untoward happened. Subsequently Nicholas Murphy wrote his report and Owen Devereux witnessed it.

In November 1910, after enquiries from Sir William Barrett as to whether there had been any more disturbances, Murphy wrote to tell him that the house was vacant, as the Redmonds had quit it the week after he had investigated it. As far as Murphy was aware, there had been no disturbances in the house until Randall went there to lodge.

Sir William Barrett eventually managed to visit Enniscorthy in November 1910, and apart from talking to Murphy, Devereux and Randall he also questioned the servant who had occupied the third bedroom. She dismissed the idea that Randall could have played a practical joke, and pointed out that the bed that moved during the manifestations was a very heavy one, with one castor missing, and that when she wished to clean the room she had to get assistance in moving it. Yet this same bed was run out into the middle of the room with Randall in it, its passage being scored into the wooden floor for all to see.

Bridget had witnessed some of the manifestations herself, including one night when another lodger, Richard Roche, had had his bedclothes pulled through the bars at the end of the bed. She had also when in her own room 'heard the bed running about the floor'. Understandably Bridget Thorpe left the house as soon as she could, but she was prepared to make a statement and to have it witnessed. So now we know that up to three occupants of the room, as well as Mr and Mrs Redmond, Nicholas Murphy, and Owen Devereux, had all witnessed events in the house and were prepared to testify to them, and to that list was now added the name of Bridget Thorpe.

Finally John Randall, described by a clergyman who knew him well as 'a thoroughly truthful and thoughtful boy', gave his own version of the events in the bedroom of the Redmonds' home. He described how on one occasion 'the bed ran out on the floor' with the three young men in it, Randall at this time being too frightened to sleep alone in the bed. He also described how he and his friends would hear 'footsteps leaving the kitchen and coming upstairs; they would stop on the landing outside the door and wouldn't come into the room . . .' He also stated that the bedclothes moved off his bed, and that he felt the bed itself moving. This kind of manifestation was repeated over a number of nights, and apart from the rappings heard in the room, noises could be heard from all over the house, including the kitchen, upper landing, and stairs.

The disturbances had become more frequent and more violent, and always happened after the light was extinguished. John Randall was not the only one pushed out of bed: it had happened to George Sinott as well, and then to both of them simultaneously. On the Saturday night before the visit of Nicholas Murphy to the room the bed turned on its side and threw both men onto the floor. John Randall also reported 'a chair dancing in the middle of the floor without a thing near it . . .'

During the constant physical and mental assault on him, John Randall, a healthy 18-year-old, affirmed that he had lost three-quarters of a stone in weight, which is hardly surprising. The three men moved out into other lodgings, and according to information from Nicholas Murphy no new manifestations occurred in their new homes. The conclusion of John Randall's statement, one feels, is a cry from the heart: 'I never believed in ghosts until that, and I think it would convince the bravest man in Ireland.'

In the preface to his account of this particular manifestation, in *Proceedings of the Society for Psychical Research*, volume 25 (1911), Sir William Barrett makes the following observation: 'The phenomena are especially sporadic, breaking out suddenly and unexpectedly, and disappearing as suddenly after a few days or weeks or months of annoyance to those concerned. They differ from hauntings in as much as they appear to be attached to an individual, usually a young person, more than to a place, or rather *to a person in a particular place.*'

As anyone who has had dealings with poltergeist phenomena knows, it is not simply a matter of dismissing the whole event as trickery, the DTs, or hallucinations. Often at the height of a particular disturbance even the most cynical of observers will find themselves powerless to prevent objects being hurled across a room, sudden and inexplicable crashes and bangs, or pools of water appearing on floors, to name but a few variations. Some observers would say that 'poltergeist' (mischievous ghost) is a well-deserved name for this phenomenon, distinguished as it is by noisy, boisterous behaviour.

Ireland has certainly had its fair share of such phenomena. In 1877 Thomas Plunkett of Enniskillen reported a mysterious disturbance in the village of Derrygonnelly, Co Fermanagh. The afflicted family consisted of a farmer and his motherless family of four girls and a boy. The eldest was about 20 and was called Maggie. The family lived in a typical Ulster cottage of one storey, which was divided into a large kitchen with two smaller rooms off it. The girls slept in one of these rooms, the farmer and his son in the other.

The manifestations were similar in some respects to the later Enniscorthy ones in that at first the noises, rappings and scrapings would usually begin when Maggie and her sisters had retired to bed. At first natural causes such as vermin were suspected, and the family were not worried unduly; and then the manifestations took on a more varied form.

Hails of stones would fall seemingly from nowhere; lamps, candles, boots and shoes were repeatedly thrown out of the house; until one of the outstanding features of the case was that the family could keep no stock of lights in the house at all: they either disappeared or were thrown out, and only by getting a neighbour to store their candles could the family have light.

Some of the neighbours suggested sending for the parish priest; others of the Methodist persuasion got the farmer to lay an open Bible on the girls' bed with a heavy stone on top. This was to no avail, for the stone was removed and placed under the book; then the Bible itself was removed from the room, and some unseen force tore seventeen leaves from it. In some distress a message was sent to Sir William (then Professor) Barrett to come from Dublin and witness matters for himself. This he did, and he later wrote in the *Dublin University Magazine* (1877) a full account of what took place.

Briefly, his observations were these. The father, son, Mr Plunkett and himself sat in the kitchen when the girls retired for the night. The door to their bedroom was left open, and Maggie, around whom much of the manifestation centred, was clearly visible as she lay on her bed over the coverlet. The knockings started fairly soon after, and appeared to emanate from the walls, ceiling and floor of the bedroom. When Professor Barrett entered the room the noise ceased, but began again once he returned to the kitchen. Mr Plunkett meanwhile had checked the outside of the cottage for any evidence. After much patient perseverance Professor Barrett found that he could enter the bedroom without the noise stopping; he could not detect any movement either from the younger children or from Maggie. On one occasion while he was observing them a large pebble fell onto the bed in front of him, having apparently materialised out of nowhere.

Baffled at the multiplicity of events, Professor Barrett sought reinforcements from Dublin in the form of an eminent scholar, the Rev Maxwell Close. Mr Close was very interested in psychic research and volunteered to come to Derrygonnelly. Barrett, Plunkett and Close returned to the farmhouse some days later, and the manifestations they witnessed were similar to those that had been seen on the earlier occasion.

The farmer told Professor Barrett that he had tried, following advice, to communicate with the entity by means of raps, and had had some success, as 'it' would respond to a given number. Barrett decided to test the theory for himself by asking it to rap out the number of fingers he had open on his hand, which was concealed in his pocket. The entity rapped out the correct number, and repeated the exercise correctly on another three occasions. Professor Barrett had communicated his request not by speech but by thought, and so the possibility of telepathic communication between the observer and the poltergeist was another area to be noted.

The unfortunate farmer, less interested in adding to the total of paranormal information than in ridding himself of his unwelcome guest, now looked to Professor Barrett and his companions for help. He asked that the clergyman should bring some spiritual pressure to bear on the entity. So Mr Close read a passage from the Bible dealing with the casting out of spirits, and then, at a further request from the farmer, he led the assembled company in prayer. The noises and the rappings, which had been quite dreadful during the scriptural passage, gradually subsided as the Lord's Prayer filled the room. By the time the last 'Amen' had been uttered the cottage was wrapped in what best can be described as a 'holy calm'.

The farmer, overcome by emotion, could hardly thank Mr Close enough for ridding his house of the manifestation that had so terrified him and his family. Mr Plunkett confirmed later that no further disturbance occurred after the visit of

Maxwell Close, and the farm and its inhabitants returned to their original obscurity and tranquillity.

In both cases, Enniskillen and Enniscorthy, Professor Barrett makes the point that the phenomena occurred mostly at night, when the person who appeared to be the focal point was at rest. In the daytime, when that person was more occupied with tasks, any manifestation that did occur was much slighter. This would bear out my own observation, that people in a state of rest or undertaking some mechanical or repetitive action that requires minimal concentration are more likely to have a paranormal experience than those whose conscious minds are fully engaged. Which brings one to the question, is this also the reason why 'ghost hunters' and the like, so busily engaged in observing and making notes, seldom see or hear anything? It is a point worth considering.

Professor Barrett makes the point that in this field of investigation, the focus of poltergeist phenomena is often a single person, a 'radiant centre' as he calls it. Most of us are aware of the connection between young people and such phenomena, although it does not occur in every case. A young person passing through puberty to adulthood could be described as being in a state of instability, and disturbances within their sphere of influence may occur because of this.

Not everyone, however, cares to rationalise the phenomenon, which while rarely dangerous can be extremely nerve-racking. A writer to the *Tipperary Star* at the beginning of the century gives an uninhibited account of his own experience in a house in the vicinity of Scotchfort, Co Mayo. The house, which was owned by relatives, had long enjoyed the reputation of being haunted; the writer's first (and last!) encounter with the lively phenomena can be appreciated. Once again it was a nightly manifestation that took place, with rattles and bangs and the breaking of china—all of which the family appeared to endure with fortitude. The terrified visitor, hearing the racket, was moved to rouse his cousin, with whom he was sharing a room, for some reassurance—only to be told: 'Ah, go to sleep now—they're only after commencing . . .' The writer's own feelings are expressed thus:

Sleep? Instantaneous death from fright was more like it! Shaking like an aspen leaf, I was not the size of a three-penny bit under the blankets, perspiring freely, with the crop on my cranium standing erect as the hair on a tooth brush. I prayed and prayed, in fact I recited all the prayers from the Key of Heaven down to Butler's penny sized Catechism, while wallop after wollop in the kitchen made the syllables and semi-syllables of the words on my tongue stagger about like drunken men. I thought I should wake up dead . . .

Morning dawned, and the kitchen was its usual silent and pristine self; but the unhappy visitor had had enough, and prudently fled. History relates that the house had had Mass said in it on several occasions, but to no avail. Finally the family too quit the house and it was left to fall down, while the locals gave the ruin a wide berth after dark.

Sir Shane Leslie, one of Ireland's best-known and best-loved writers on the paranormal, cites in his *Ghost Book* a mildly humorous sectarian element to be encountered among Irish poltergeists:

> In June 1910 I performed the pilgrimage to Lough Derg with two young Catholic students . . . We did the pilgrimage with fervour and returned walking from the lake to the village of Pettigo in Co. Donegal. As the village was on family property I suggested that we should sleep the night in the Agency. Here I slept as I had often slept in the past, the sleep of the just. But my companions, who had deserved every consideration from Morpheus . . . were troubled and tossed and torn by a ghost who stripped the bedclothes from them. By morning they had not slept a wink . . .

The young travellers confided their tale to the local publican, a Mr Flood, who informed them that they had probably fallen foul of the Protestant spirit of the late agent, James McCullough, who had died two years previously. Sir Shane remarks: 'Poor James' feelings can be understood at finding two Catholic pilgrims in his bed . . .'

To those of us who live in the north of Ireland, the prospect of a 'Protestant poltergeist' is quite conceivable!

A possible case of 'diabolical intent', if one is to accept the word of local clergy, was the poltergeist manifestation that happened at Coonian, near Brookeborough, Co Fermanagh. It was a case that became as well known in the annals of Irish hauntings as the Derrygonnelly poltergeist.

Once more there were young people involved, this time teen-age girls. The Catholic clergy became involved in this case at an early stage, and much of the detailed information about the case comes from them. One priest sent to investigate described how he saw 'the shape of a human form' under the sheets on an empty bed. The bedclothes on the girls' bed were thrown across the room, and the disturbance continued even after the priest had laid hold of the girls to ascertain if they were phy-sically responsible for the movement of the clothes. There were 'spitting noises' and hisses—and, even more surprising, the whistling at times of recognisable tunes.

It was then that the church brought out the big guns. Mass was said in the house and holy water was sprinkled in all the rooms. This simply provoked more disturbances, such as ham-mering and knocking and the dousing of lights both inside and outside the house. The entity would, on occasion, answer questions by raps; and asked in the presence of a horse dealer how many horse dealers were there, the entity rapped loudly under his chair, the lights on his trap outside were put out, and the pony became nearly demented with fear.

In one experiment a dog was pushed in under the bed where much of the manifestation took place, whereupon it was thrown out bodily by some unseen force. The terrified animal fled from the room, and no amount of coaxing could get it to come in again.

By this time Coonian was the talk of the countryside, and clerics of almost every persuasion had visited the Murphys. Sir Shane Leslie, who had first-hand experience of the case, spent some time with the family and in the company of Father S., the priest appointed by the bishop to assist in the expulsion of the Murphys' unwelcome guest.

As they stood one evening in a room in the farmhouse below the loft, which was used for storing fodder, they heard the tramping of feet above their heads, which Sir Shane likened to 'the footfall of a large dog or sheep'. He then climbed the outside steps to the loft and found nothing, although his companion below heard the tramping continuing even while Sir Shane investigated. Later something was to 'rush past them' in that lower room and 'go into the ground'.

At dawn on that day the bedclothes in the room began to move up and down in an agitated fashion. By now the rest of the family had come from the kitchen into the bedroom. Sir Shane Leslie takes up the account:

> The movements of the bedclothes were gradually getting more vigorous, pronounced and defined. The whole thing resembled a form of a person lying diagonally across the bed in his or her death agony. The centre where the clothes were heaving most was where the chest would be. Soon we could hear the heavy breathing, the gurgling in the throat, the symptoms of pain. It resembled what country people would call 'a hard death'. From the time they came from the kitchen the whole death scene occupied ten minutes at the least. Finally the movements and the death symptoms ceased and the room was as quiet as the grave.

This harrowing experience was repeated again before other witnesses. Some of the manifestations seemed to centre around the eldest daughter, Annie, who attracted the most vigorous knockings on the bed if she lay on it, as well as a 'rushing sound'.

Finally one of the attending priests, having been out on a sick visit, took the Blessed Sacrament into the bedroom, and taking out the pyx made the sign of the cross over the bed. The disturbance following this act of piety was most impressive, and those in the house were terrified; but the valiant priest stood his ground, and at long last the 'entity' was expelled.

Overcome by their experience, the Murphy family emigrated to America and were troubled no more. The clergy, however, did sustain some injury: one priest had a nervous collapse, one contracted meningitis, and another Bell's palsy. The bishop of the diocese was convinced that the manifestations were of diabolical origin, although why a full exorcism was not carried out was never fully explained.

The whole idea of a 'radiant centre' or 'nucleus' being the focal point for these violent bouts of energy has to be considered along with other possibilities. We are bound to ask such questions as, do we all have the capacity, by a release of psychokinetic energy, to produce a poltergeist effect, and are we talking about the same kind of energy release that may have been harnessed by ancient man, to perform weight-lifting feats for example? There is also the possible power of the discarnate mind to consider; and if this power is undiminished for some time after dissolution then this too could be the focal point for poltergeist activity. More contentious perhaps is the idea that there really are noisy, boisterous entities on the perimeter of our world. As with so much of the paranormal, we need to keep an open mind.

Certainly the poltergeist phenomenon is one of Ireland's 'front runners' in the paranormal stakes, and documented accounts of it occur over a long time, although the nineteenth and early twentieth centuries possess some of the best-attested accounts.

In Drogheda in the 1890s a Mrs Weir and her husband were forced to leave their home because 'something' repeatedly hurled heavy objects at her in the seclusion of her bedroom; while in south Dublin from August 1844 to January 1845 stones were hurled at an unidentified house and an amount of damage was sustained. This manifestation was accompanied by footsteps, and the police and more than twenty witnesses testified to it.

As for poltergeist manifestations in my own experience, I have come across several cases where there were partial poltergeistic phenomena; and apart from those cases related elsewhere in this book there are two that stand out in my mind.

The first case was that of Mrs R. of Belfast. In 1969 I was asked to help investigate a series of incidents in which she was involved. Mrs R. lived with her family in a modern semi-detached house in north Belfast. I was put in touch with her through the good offices of a journalist friend, George, to whom she had gone for help. The basic information she had passed on to him was that her life, and that of her home and family, appeared to have been taken over by some unseen and menacing presence.

It was a cold wintry night when George and I made our way across the city to be greeted with relief by Mrs R. and her husband, who, having made us comfortable in front of a cheerful fire with a cup of tea, proceeded to tell us all that had happened so far.

They were an English couple, only lately arrived from across the water, and they had been well pleased and happy in their new home at first. The area was cheerful and well served with shops and schools, and it was also very handy to Mr R.'s work. Everything was fine for two or three weeks; then Mrs R. began to feel that although the rest of the family had left for work or school, she was still not alone in the house.

At first the feeling was vague, just the sense of someone standing behind her, then a fleeting pressure like a hand on her shoulder and the ever-growing sensation of being watched. Mrs R. put it down to an unfamiliar environment and her nerves, but then she started to fear for her sanity as she began to hear a voice that called to her by name. The atmosphere in the house was also beginning to tell on her two young children and of course on her husband, who was miserably aware that the nature of his work meant that he was out of the house all hours of the day and night. The nightmarish presence grew stronger, until Mrs R. could get no peace. At night the presence would wake her; and then the children began to complain of a shadowy figure in their bedrooms. There were thumps and bangs, and the light-fittings, all newly installed, began to behave in an unpredictable fashion. Switches on the walls would click into the 'on' position unaided, and this happened with such frequency that Mr R. (an engineer) was forced to go over the wiring in an attempt to find a solution. He found everything in perfect order, but still the lights clicked on and off at will.

After about a month of these events Mrs R. heard of my interest from a friend, who said that he would contact George at his newspaper office and ask him to speak to me. As we sat in that pleasant sitting-room discussing what might be the best thing to do, it was hard to credit that anything at all was wrong. But two incidents occurred while we were there: both George and myself heard a distinct knocking on or near the front door, although when the door was opened there was no-one there. A few moments after this George remarked that despite the fire he could feel a distinct area of cold between us. We were at this time sitting on the settee and separated by two to three feet. After a moment Mrs R. exclaimed nervously, 'It's here! I can feel it!' While we saw nothing it was patently obvious how frightened our hostess had become. It was also noticeable that Mrs R. frequently referred to the presence as 'her', and she later confirmed that she thought the presence was female, giving as evidence the fact that the hand she felt on her shoulder was 'like a woman's hand'.

After a few minutes she became easier; and after undertaking to help in any way we could we left, promising to keep in touch by telephone and to visit again in a day or two.

My first task was to examine the area on which the housing estate was built and to try to find out what may have stood there before the building of the new houses. My investigation revealed very little, apart from the fact that an old house had once occupied part of the site. This house had been of no historical interest, and as far as I could find out no crime of violence had taken place in the vicinity. Discreet enquiries among the neighbours also revealed that no-one else had had any 'trouble' in their homes.

During the next two to three weeks I kept in close touch with Mrs R., and it became obvious that the manifestations were becoming more pronounced. Items in the kitchen and store cupboard were interfered with, there were continued knocks and bangs, and the lights still flicked on and off. More significantly there were the voices, as well as the direct information that was coming from Mrs R., who was proving to be a natural medium.

The entity told her its name was May or Mary, and that it was afraid. It repeatedly said 'pray for me', or alternatively asked for a priest. As Mrs R. was not a Catholic I undertook to make contact with the local clergy, and was surprised and saddened at the lack of sympathy and understanding my request received. The reverend gentleman I approached had only one practical suggestion to offer: that I should get Mrs R. a 'head doctor', and maybe avail myself of his services too! As for the hapless 'Mary' she could seemingly shift for herself, as she was not within his pastoral care! Fortunately for all concerned I did find a more sympathetic and understanding ear when I approached a local medium and her husband, who undertook to help, but in the strictest confidence.

The medium was as good as her word, and a séance was held in Mrs R.'s bedroom, where Mary was persuaded to tell the whole story. It seemed that she was indeed the daughter of the one-time occupant of the old house that had stood on the site. Her father, a typical Victorian bully, had ensured that all her life his daughter had gone in fear of him. Eventually the father had died, while Mary, who had only been in her twenties, died shortly after him. Now she confided that she had feared and hated her father in life, and in death was terrified of meeting him again. At least this was the explanation given to the medium for why she had stayed close to the old house and, lonely and frightened, had transferred her affections to Mrs R., whom she described as 'the only friend I have ever known'.

After one or two sessions the medium persuaded Mary to leave her confined existence, and with help, this fearful and pathetic personality was persuaded to move forward into her own place. No-one who witnessed these sessions could fail to be moved by the loneliness expressed by Mary as she communicated through the body of the medium.

From that time on there were no more problems for Mrs R. or her family, although she was anxious that Mary should be all right and did not wish to desert her. Shortly after this episode Mr R. returned to work in England, and the story of Mary was concluded. Certainly I heard no more from the family, so I must assume that Mary had turned her face towards the light.

There are other explanations of poltergeist activity of course, and for the manifesting of 'Mary' I am only offering one explanation: that we were dealing with a disturbance whose focal point was a discarnate personality. It could equally be true that Mrs R. was externalising some facet of her own unconscious and that not 'Mary' but Mrs R. was the centre of the manifestation. Even if that were so it would have been difficult to prove it in so short a time, and virtually impossible without going into Mrs R.'s personal history. Her husband had assured us that nothing like this had ever happened to his wife before and that she had always been a tranquil and contented person. It was possible, he conceded, that she missed England and her family and friends, but not unbearably so. The children, both under 8, had only had minimal involvement with the manifestation and seemed well adjusted and happy.

For me the most memorable part of the whole episode was when Mrs R. turned to me after the final séance and said, 'She came to me for help; I don't want that poor lonely soul to be frightened any more'—a lesson in Christian charity that contrasted sharply with the clerical response we had received and that says much for the generous nature of the woman in question.

My last account of poltergeist activity is of events in Whitehead, Co Antrim, in 1982. It is a case that has many classic features, and again, thanks to the perseverance of the people involved, it has a happy ending.

The mother involved, whom we shall call Veronica, moved into her home in Whitehead with her two teenage children, 13-year-old Paul and 14-year-old Catherine. What the family was not aware of at the time was that the previous occupants had left the house after disturbances that had given them sleepless nights. With the advent of the teenage children the disturbances became slightly worse at first, then gradually increased in intensity. The focal point was the bedroom of the daughter, Catherine, who endured thumps and bangs, posters torn off the walls, and the moving of books from the bed-table. Sometimes her guitar would twang away to itself, as did the family's electric organ. Other common events were the lights being switched on and off, door handles being turned, and footsteps in the house.

The unfortunate girl was losing not only a lot of sleep but study time as well; and then, like Mrs R. in our previous story, she began to hear vague and indistinct voices. Unlike Mrs R., however, Veronica consulted her Methodist minister, who took her complaints very seriously and offered to bless the house. The daughter, more mature for her years than one might expect, was anxious about the visit of the minister; she felt it would only make matters worse, and eventually she was proved right. Not dismayed, her mother invited in turn the Church of Ireland rector and the Roman Catholic curate. Both men did a thorough job of blessing every nook and cranny, but were in effect no more successful than the Methodist parson, and the manifestations continued unabated.

By now the mother, with a friend who had some experience of psychic research, had come to the conclusion that whatever the entity was it wasn't demoniac. Therefore it seemed a logical assumption that whoever or whatever it was needed help. Through a mutual friend the women contacted a non-conformist minister who had some experience of 'rescue circles', and they found him to be willing but without a medium at that time. In the meantime a local clairvoyant was contacted who had some experience of mediumship as well, and he offered to send his 'guide' to the house to see what might be learned. The information that was passed on was that the house had been occupied by a very disturbed personality, a woman, who had died but who was not aware of her discarnate state.

This information was subsequently verified by a neighbour who explained that a widow with a subnormal child had lived in the house. The woman, a Mrs D., had doted on the child, and it had been a great shock to the neighbourhood when Mrs D. was taken ill and died. The boy was removed to the local care centre for the mentally handicapped.

With this amount of information the two women decided to hold a séance in the house while the daughter was away on holiday. With Catherine absent there was a noticeable drop in activity, which would lead one to suppose that the teenager supplied the motivating energy to a large extent. Her mother had surmised, perhaps accurately, that the bedroom occupied by her daughter was the one that had been occupied by the handicapped child.

Two other friends were called in to help, one of whom, Michael, was in fact a teacher of the mentally handicapped. Two days before Catherine left to go on holiday matters became dramatically worse, culminating in the family having to spend the night downstairs while footsteps and a 'wailing sound' assaulted their ears. Understandably the seekers after the truth were somewhat disconcerted by all the commotion, but not put off from holding their own enquiry.

The method employed is not one that I would approve of in the hands of amateurs. The four people used a wineglass and letters to attempt to contact the entity—a very dangerous undertaking. Nevertheless after half an hour or so they began to get answers from the glass. It seemed that 'Mrs Dixon' was the name of the widow mooted by the wineglass, and the group asked her some questions. The entity was glad to talk to someone, and in return the group reassured 'Mrs Dixon' about the child's wellbeing. Finally the first exhausting session came to an end, and the group promised to contact her again if the entity in turn would leave the family in peace. This promise, seemingly, was forthcoming. A week later the group met again and contact was re-established, without the original difficulties. Michael, the teacher, had news of the child's transfer to a children's home by the sea, and could reassure 'Mrs Dixon' that all was well with him. Then they had the delicate task of breaking it to the entity that she was now dis-carnate. To their surprise they learned that she knew, but she was afraid, and unsure of what she should do—this confused state may well account for the upsurge in activity before the séance, as the personality attempted to come to terms with its changed state. The group pointed out the advantages of being reunited with loved ones, and that the house now held nothing for her, that she would find peace and love in her own place.

I quote from a letter I received from a member of the group afterwards:

> I suggested she should turn her back on us and look beyond the house. Was there a light in that direction? There was. Could she see people she had once known? She could. Then all she had to do was to walk away from the house and towards them and they would take care of her. With that the glass stopped dead—it was as though the life went out of it—and although we kept our fingers on it for several minutes it did not move again. Mrs Dixon had gone!

When Catherine returned to her bedroom she reported that it felt 'empty', and from that day to this the house had no more manifestations.

Whatever reservations I have about the use of the glass and letters, it would be unfair to dismiss the result as being a product of some shared hallucinatory experience. This group had sat down with the aim of helping someone who they felt needed their help, and as far as one can judge they appear to have been successful. But such experiment is not for the innocent or inexperienced; and while their guardian angels may have been on the alert that is not always the case, nor is it always the end of poltergeist activity.

The Woman
on the Pavement

In the late 1960s I had a telephone call from a Mrs Donnelly, who wanted to tell me about an unusual event that had happened to her some months previously. She had been travelling on a Belfast city bus when on the pavement near to a bus-stop she saw a face she recognised. 'It was of a girl who had been a friend and workmate for years,' she said; 'the girl had turned from looking in a shop window in Royal Avenue, and as the bus drew away from the stop she looked straight into the bus at me.' Mrs Donnelly's reaction was predictable. 'I got a funny, cold sensation, and I thought that I must be dreaming, for I knew the girl had died a fortnight before, after a long illness; indeed I had followed her coffin.'

I pressed my informant for more details. 'Could you say that she looked quite normal?' I asked. Mrs Donnelly confirmed this. 'Oh, she was there all right; a bit pale maybe and tired-looking, but she was wearing a coat I knew well, and there was no doubt that when she looked into the bus, she saw me, for our eyes met.' After a pause I asked Mrs Donnelly what she thought she had seen. She hesitated and then replied, 'I think I saw her ghost.'

The idea that apparitions are simply manifestations of the dead that sometimes appear to chosen people among the living is a simplistic one. If the study of apparitions over the past eighty years has taught us anything it is that nothing in the field of paranormal investigation, and especially the study of apparitions, is ever straightforward. It is an area fraught with complications. Supporting evidence for this can be found in the reports and proceedings of that eminent body, the Society for Psychical Research, whose careful and painstaking work over the years has simply revealed the tip of the iceberg in theories and half-theories about the nature of apparitions. As

F.W. Myers, himself a most painstaking researcher, commented ruefully, 'whatever else indeed a ghost may be, it is one of the most complex phenomena in nature.'

Apparitions manifest themselves in a variety of ways and situations. They can be representational of persons living or dead, they may be substantial or insubstantial, whole or partial, and seen by day or night. The traditional association of ghosts with churchyards and ancient sites is firmly knocked on the head by the range of sightings in council houses, caravans, cinemas, and even, in my experience, a public lavatory! Normally apparitions are not given to talking, and they can be of anything known in material form on this planet—a bird, a house, a cat, or a tree—although for the purpose of this chapter I am assuming that the term 'apparition' applies only to those in human form.

Just as apparitions take a wide variety of forms, so too do the theories advanced for the reason for seeing apparitions in the first place, and obviously one cannot be too dogmatic about the experiencing of such a phenomenon. In the case of Mrs Donnelly and her city pavement experience one can only hazard an opinion. This could have been a visual projection of an image from Mrs Donnelly's subconscious. She was in a relaxed state sitting on the bus, with nothing particular occupying her mind. It is not impossible that at that point the subliminal level of her mind projected the image of her dead friend into a setting that would have been natural and appropriate.

This theory could not be applied in exactly the same fashion to another Belfast woman, who in May 1961 wrote to tell me of an apparition she had seen nearly thirty years earlier, in October 1938 in Alexandra Park, Belfast. Mrs E.E. wrote:

I was returning home from shopping one afternoon and was passing along Castleton Gardens, beside the railings of Alexandra Park—there was no-one else about at the time. Just then I noticed the figure of a woman coming out of Jubilee Avenue from the Antrim Road; she crossed the road and went into the Park, I watched her walking down the path, when suddenly she disappeared. To my surprise when I reached the gates they were locked; the time was almost five o'clock. When I noticed her she was wearing a Black Shawl with what looked like a white skirt, then I remembered that the Spinners in the mills wore all round white aprons before 1914. It was no human being who could walk through closed gates and disappear half way down the path.

This time the observer sees someone unknown to her, but much as in the case of Mrs Donnelly her mind is at rest as she strolls home along a familiar route. Did Mrs E.E. 'tune in' to the aetheric record of a spinner from the mill also walking her familiar way home? It is possible that what Mrs E.E. saw was a 'recording' of a commonplace event and to which her own ESP equipment reacted, thus enabling her to 'see' the figure of the spinner. If this is the solution, bearing in mind the theory that sight and sound are never 'lost', merely translated to another dimension, then this was not really a ghost but a moving picture of an actual event whose 'negative image' had suddenly become 'positive'.

A daylight apparition of ostensibly solid proportions was reported to me in the early 1970s by a Co Antrim baker. The incident happened one afternoon towards the end of the last war. The baker, living in the countryside to the west of Belfast, was going home for his tea when he saw a man walking briskly towards him along the road. The baker, a Mr K., was at this time passing the wall of a farmyard that bounded one side of the lane for a little distance. As the man got nearer to him Mr K. thought he seemed familiar, and as they passed one another Mr K. bade him a courteous 'Good evening'. The man made no reply, and appeared to be earnestly studying the farm and the outbuildings. It wasn't until he was some yards past that Mr K. realised why the man looked familiar. 'When he was gone past I realised who it was, and the flesh crept on my bones. It was the farmer who had owned the farm I was just passing and who I knew slightly. I had been at his funeral Mass only two weeks before.' When I asked Mr K. for his next reaction he stared soberly into the fire for a moment, then said: 'Sure I turned and looked after him, but I knew that I would see no-one there, and with the wall on the one side and the hedge on the other he couldn't have turned off—so I raised my cap and said a wee prayer for him . . .'

In the tradition of rural Co Down this confrontation would

have been described as seeing the 'fetch' of the deceased; and the belief that they returned home, perhaps for one last look at familiar things, is a common explanation. But once again one is confronted by the idea that Mr K.'s own unconscious mind had indulged in 'projection by association'. He was after all passing the dead man's home, and the funeral was still relatively fresh in his memory, if not in the conscious mind. Yet one hesitates to dismiss the older belief, for such is the strength of the human spirit that to have 'one last look' is not such a bizarre idea, and is one, I suspect, with which most of us would have a fellow-feeling.

In more recent times the 'troubles' in Northern Ireland have produced some paranormal incidents, if not as many as one might have expected or at least have expected to be reported to interested parties. One can only speculate on the natural reticence in the light of the welter of tragedy and heartache that has been our daily portion.

One report that did emerge was retailed to me in 1980 after an evening lecture to a women's organisation in a border town in Co Down. The witness, a clergyman, spoke of a Mr O'F. who had been driving home along the road between Warrenpoint and Newry, Co Down. The time had been about nine o'clock on an autumn evening about six months before. The road where the incident happened is a broad modern highway bounded on one side by the shore of Carlingford Lough. The witness was alone in the car and was listening to the radio as he approached Narrowater Castle, a square battlemented tower built around 1560 by the Magennis chiefs, who held it until they forfeited their estates in the seventeenth century, whereupon it passed to the Hall family, who placed it in state charge in 1956. Suddenly ahead of him Mr O'F. saw a powerful light being swung in a wide arc from beside the road. Immediately he slowed down and prepared to stop for what he took to be a road block.

Indeed as he drew to a halt he saw, beside the road in the shadow of the trees and at the entrance to the castle, a number of soldiers carrying rifles, and closer to him one soldier in combat dress holding a torch. Mr O'F. wound down his window and waited for the soldier to come round to his side of the car. The soldier asked for his driving licence, and for him to open the boot. The witness complied by opening his door and moving round to the rear of the car. Mr O'F. is then reported to have said that he felt 'most peculiar' and that 'a great shiver ran over me.' He became convinced that something was, in his own words, terribly wrong. He stood back to allow the soldier to examine the boot, and then he realised that there was no-one standing beside him. His driving licence lay on the ground at the driver's door.

Three similar incidents were reported either to family or local papers, one involving three young women in a car, and all of them occurred between June 1980 and March 1981. In each case the witness is alleged to have said that he or she was 'flagged down as though for a security check', and that one soldier came to the car, although others could be seen. Only Mr O'F. claimed that the soldier spoke to him. One needs little reminder that only a few yards from this spot, in August 1979, eighteen soldiers met their deaths in a particularly barbaric IRA ambush.

Again one has to examine the evidence as it was reported. In the case of Mr O'F. he was alone in his car, his mind no doubt in that state of 'rest' common to experienced motorists in familiar surroundings. Projected hallucinations among the motoring public are not uncommon; and I can quote a personal experience.

Some years ago a colleague and myself were returning from Dublin after taking part in a television broadcast. We were travelling along a stretch of the Dublin road well known to us, and in broad daylight. Suddenly the car screeched to a halt as my companion gave a spirited demonstration of an 'emergency stop'. I knew precisely why he had, as I had seen dangling at windscreen height, in front of the car, what seemed to be a power cable. I had ducked instinctively as the car ground to a halt. We both got out, a trifle shaken by our narrow escape, only to discover that there was absolutely nothing across the road. It was completely clear and there was nothing in the immediate vicinity that we could have possibly construed as a fallen power line. Yet we had both seen it and, judging from our reactions, at about the same time. The question that interested me on that occasion, after I'd recovered my breath, was, did we both hallucinate and see an identical projection, or did one of us hallucinate and the other pick up the message telepathically? There was no way to prove the hypothesis one way or the other.

To return to Mr O'F. on the Warrenpoint road: the flashing of a torch by police or soldiers is a common experience on Ulster roads, as is the sight of a group of soldiers at a checkpoint. The only oddity he recollected later was that he didn't remember seeing any military vehicles in the vicinity, which was unusual. As to the rest of the sequence of events that occurred, everything was in order, until he opened his boot.

Then there is the statement of Mr O'F. to his parish priest. He complained of 'feeling cold'; 'an enormous shiver ran down my back'—and then the horrified realisation that he was alone and that the grass verges were bare, while his driving licence lay on the ground at his feet.

How does one attempt to analyse this information? For me it was made all the more frustrating because I was hearing it at second hand, the witness declining to tell the tale to anyone else. There were certain aspects of the information that could tie in with events reported from various parts of the world and akin to the universal 'hitch-hiker' myth. Yet it wasn't as simple as that, nor could I dismiss the report. The Warrenpoint ambush was of course common knowledge, and there must have been few people who passed by that spot who would not have had some thoughts about it in their mind, Mr O'F. included. Certainly the framework for the experience could already have existed in his unconscious, and indeed on one or two occasions Mr O'F. may have been stopped at a real checkpoint on that road.

All things considered, then, are we somewhere along the road to being able to describe this incident not as a paranormal experience but as a hallucinatory event complete with 'voice'? Or is there still room to suppose that this could have been a paranormal experience with some clairaudience involved? Certainly the feeling of cold is consistent with some extra-sensory experience, and in that heightened state of consciousness Mr O'F. may have experienced both clairvoyance and clairaudience. If we simply assume it was a trick of the unconscious mind, then we also have to ask, why on that particular night, and why in such detail?

There is another possible explanation. It is a fairly logical assumption that if an incarnate mind can perform acts of projection, as we are suggesting, then where a great deal of physical and emotional trauma has been experienced, could there not be a residual energy concentrated in that spot, which, given a suitable vehicle of communication, could trigger a paranormal incident? Might not the collective energy of a group of discarnate minds generate sufficient power to effect the materialisation of forms for a brief moment, and to clothe that sequence in the semblance of normality, including a voice? The unconscious recollections of Mr O'F., combined with the use of his mind as a 'vehicle' for whatever energy was present, may have created the road-block scene. Again one is suggesting a kind of re-run of a silent recording, but in this case there is also the apparent involvement of the witness in the activity.

In an entirely different setting, an apparition of a soldier was seen by a motorist on the road between Banbridge and Loughbrickland, Co Down. Mr D., a bank manager, was on his way from his home in Hillsborough, Co Down, to his office in Newry at about half-past eight on a fine June morning. (This was not the new dual carriageway, but the old road to Newry.)

About three miles out of Banbridge he saw beside the road, a few yards from a gate into a field, a young soldier, apparently waiting for someone.

> The soldier was wearing a khaki greatcoat and forage cap, he had a kitbag slung over his shoulder, and gaiters or puttees over his boots. The reason I can be so specific is that I slowed down as I approached, in case it was an army check-point. But as I passed him he gave no sign that he noticed me, and he carried no rifle, just the kitbag. He was quite substantial and normal in appearance, if a bit pale . . . I was thinking about other things, so I was a good hundred yards past him when the full impact of what I had seen hit me. I looked into the rear-view mirror, but the soldier had gone.

Mr D. stopped the car and reversed back almost to the gate. He got out and looked up and down the road and into the field, but there was no-one about. He was emphatic in his assertion that no vehicle had passed him and that he had had a clear view of the road for about a hundred yards. He admitted that the soldier could have gone into the field and hidden, but to what end?

His reaction to the incident had been based on a number of discrepancies in the soldier's dress and behaviour. In the first place, soldiers in Northern Ireland seldom stroll casually about solo on country roads; they are always armed, and for the most part they wear combat gear. This man on a mild June morning was wearing a greatcoat and a forage cap, and carrying a kitbag but no rifle: hardly the accoutrements of a modern soldier! Mr D. repeated his assertion that the uniform reminded him of 'the last war', in which he himself had served. 'I know what I saw, and I described it to my wife in detail.' He was also emphatic that the soldier was not hitching a lift, but appeared to be waiting for someone.

As far as I could ascertain, Mr D. had the soldier in his sight for about thirty seconds or a little less—as he approached him, and as he passed him—but when he checked in the rear-view mirror the soldier had gone.

If one compares this incident with the Warrenpoint Road event one sees that Mr D. was also alone in his car, but it was early in the morning and broad daylight. There were no accompanying figures and no link between Mr D. and what he saw. It was the incongruity that alerted the witness and nothing else; had there been two soldiers armed and in combat dress, Mr D. would have thought no more of it.

So what conclusions can we come to? As a middle-aged man and an ex-serviceman Mr D. would have been aware of the dress of a Second World War soldier. His mind could have selected an image from his unconscious and projected it onto the background of the country road, for some obscure reason best known to itself. Another possibility is that some trivial and forgotten incident in Mr D.'s mind that had to do with a soldier standing beside the road could have been triggered and projected. A third possibility is that at some time in the past a soldier *had* stood on that spot and had been waiting for someone, and the aetheric record of that incident remained and was picked up by Mr D.'s extrasensory perception, and the incident was 're-run' on that June morning. Whether the soldier was dead or alive at the time that Mr D. saw him is irrelevant: the witness merely tuned in to a very common wartime occurrence.

This last explanation, however incomplete and frustrating (because there is no corroboration of the story), does appear to me to be the most likely, bearing in mind that Mr D. had no vested interest whatever in making up such a trivial tale. There was no historical evidence connected to the sighting, and no-one else had ever seen the soldier as far as we know. So in essence the 'soldier on the Dublin road' must remain another uncorroborated, subjective experience in the annals of paranormal investigation.

A less pleasant account concerning the apparition of a soldier was mooted abroad by a local journalist. It concerned the apparition seen in one of Belfast's blocks of high-rise flats. In 1971 two soldiers were killed by an explosion in a rubbish-chute on one of the floors of the tower block. Later, witnesses complained of disturbances in the form of moans and cries of pain accompanied by footsteps in the vicinity of the rubbish-chute. The apparition occurred in the early hours of the morning and was reported by a resident of the flats, who did not wish to be identified. She said she saw a young soldier standing alone on the staircase in what appeared to be a very distressed condition. 'It was quite dark, and for a moment I thought that I was imagining things; then when I got up close I saw him quite clearly. All of a sudden he seemed to float off into mid-air and vanish.'

In this instance more than one witness spoke of noises, but there was only one report of an apparition. The belief that disturbances occur at the sites of violent actions is an ancient and respected one. It would be too simplistic to label an experience such as this an 'unquiet spirit', although that point of view will have its adherents. As F.W. Myers pointed out when he discussed the nature of phantoms, there is little evidence to actually connect discarnate personalities with the hallucinatory effects often experienced. It is impossible, for obvious reasons, to say that discarnate personalities, if such there be, will favour certain localities, even though there may have been a connection in life. Equally one cannot rule out the possibility—which is why the study of the paranormal requires a very open and undogmatic approach.

One ingredient present in the kind of report received from the flats and that was not present in the case of the soldier on the Banbridge Road would be the degree of hearsay that would have existed already among the residents of the flats. No-one is suggesting that the reports were not given in good faith, but there may have been perfectly rational explanations for a number of the noises heard, and they would have needed investigation in the first place. This does not remove the possibility that some paranormal manifestation did take place, and in particular there may have been among the witnesses a 'sensitive' whose awareness may have been in a heightened state as a result of being in contact with some residual source of energy.

It would be an unforgivable transgression to be writing a book about the paranormal in Ireland and not to mention the Grey Lady of Lambeg, Co Antrim. Her appearances in the village at irregular intervals have been going on for generations. Her traditional walk was between Lambeg House, known locally as 'the Chains' (because of the posts and chains around the perimeter of the property), and Lambeg parish church, which stands on the hill outside the village. The house, alas, is no more, having been burned down in an arson attack in the 1970s. Even the tree under which King Billy is supposed to have rested his horse is no more, but the road that follows the line of the river and goes up the hill to the church is much as it has always been.

The introduction to the Ordnance Survey of 1837 says that Lambeg churchyard was the site of a nunnery, the ruins being removed in 1824. In 1806 the Rev Edmund Cupples wrote that there had once been a monastic site beside the church and a nunnery across the river, and that a connecting passage had existed. The apparition of a nun is said to appear from the side of Lambeg House and walk the road to the church, where a part of the old graveyard is known as the Nuns' Garden.

The tradition that there was an underground passage leading from one building to another on this ancient site is also told about Lambeg House. In this instance the passage was said to run from the house to the church, but no evidence of such a passage has ever come to light.

The early State Papers of 1601 contain a reference to a

[104]

Franciscan house on this site, and to this day the house opposite the site of Lambeg House is called Priory House. The story of the 'grey lady' does therefore have some historical background.

I lived in the village myself for five years and from time to time reports of 'the lady' would reach me. One villager returning home in the early hours of an October morning saw 'the form of a woman' emerge from the shadow of Lambeg House, and much to his consternation she glided after him for a short distance up Church Hill. Another man walking on Church Hill was also joined by the 'grey lady', who vanished through the gate into the old churchyard.

The most bizarre account I had was from a plain-speaking Scot who lived not in the village proper but within comfortable walking distance of the church. He told me that early one morning he saw the nun superimposed on the branch of a tree outside his house, and that on another occasion he had seen the head and shoulders of a nun looking out of an upstairs window in the house. Whether this was the same 'grey lady' is a matter for conjecture, because there had been a history of disturbances in his house in Sandy Lane, to which I can bear witness. These took the form of a front door opening and shutting and footsteps upstairs, to which the dogs of the household took great exception.

Two later events were reported to me in the 1980s. One occurred in September 1979 when a woman with two children was climbing the hill and she saw the nun, the time being about eight o'clock; the figure crossed the road in the direction of the churchyard gate and went inside. As far as my informant could judge, the children did not see the apparition.

The other informant actually lived on Church Hill, almost opposite the church. She maintained that the apparition of a nun haunted her house and that she had seen her in an upstairs room; at the same time books and other objects were moved about. My own home in the village was believed to occupy the site of the guest-house belonging to the monastery. We also experienced footsteps both inside and outside the bungalow, as did our neighbour. My young son complained once or twice of the man who walked through his room and took his leave via the window, which far from causing my 5-year-old to be frightened seemed rather to occasion a certain amount of merriment!

If one collects together the information on the 'grey lady' and attempts to impose a pattern on the appearances, it poses certain difficulties. The apparition, now part of the folk tradition of the area, seems to have wandered irregularly, sometimes at quite a distance from her traditional walk between house and church. It is possible of course that there is more than one 'grey lady' and that a certain amount of confusion has arisen because of the similarities in the manifestations. There does appear to be a tenuous connection between Lambeg House and the old churchyard beside the parish church, while the house in Sandy Lane stands beside what was once a right of way over the fields from the church, and so presumably could have been used by the community at an earlier time.

If one also considers the fact that the village appears to be situated on what was once a substantial monastic site, which has in one way or another been continually occupied for the last eight hundred years, then it is hardly surprising that echoes from the past still come down to us at Lambeg.

All Creatures Great and Small

There was a belief among the Irish country people that domestic animals possessed the gift of knowing all about their human masters and mistresses. They listened to us, divined our expressions, and read our thoughts. In the realm of the paranormal, animals are often gifted with far more perception than we ourselves, partly, one supposes, because they are not hampered by logic or a desire to rationalise. Therefore they see and hear whatever is there to be seen and heard, and eventually, when they themselves are in dissolution, do not appear to be hindered at all by the dogma that the creatures that are deemed lesser than ourselves are also deemed to possess neither a spiritual quality nor a soul. But those of us who have encountered the apparitions of animals know that just as everything in our world that has life can manifest itself in another state, so can these creatures that love and trust us in life.

Inevitably the legends and superstitions that surround a variety of animals in Ireland can make the disentanglement of genuine paranormal experience from the occult and the faerie that much more difficult. Some instances of course can exist simultaneously in more than one category, depending on the circumstances, just as the *bean sí* may be both a fairy figure and a paranormal experience.

One such tradition that belongs both to folklore and the paranormal is the belief that surrounds the howling of a dog. It is said that if a dog howls near the house of a sick person, 'all hope of his recovery may be given up, and the patient himself sinks into despair, knowing that his doom is sealed.' I have had several accounts over the years of animals howling or whimpering at the approach of death to a member of the family; in fact some Eastern traditions hold that a dog sees the face of Death, and cowers at the approach of the Dark

[107]

Angel. Thomas Hardy's dog is said to have seen death on the face of one of his master's great friends and refused to approach him.

I can only vouch for one personal experience of this phenomenon. A near relative of mine who had been seriously ill for some time but who at the time appeared to be stable, had as a companion a small black poodle. On the night before the woman died, while the human watchers could detect no change, the small dog who had lain so faithfully beside the bed each night for months gave a loud whine and made frantic attempts to leave the room. It refused to re-enter the sick room and instead lay outside the door whimpering for most of the night. At noon the following day his mistress breathed her last, and the dog sorrowfully rose and made his way to his basket in the kitchen and refused to be consoled. The sudden decline into death had taken the rest of us wholly by surprise, but the poodle knew hours beforehand what was to happen.

The belief that dogs can see death is an ancient one. Even today the sound of a dog howling mournfully in the small hours of the morning can send a shiver down one's spine, no matter how 'modern' or 'logical' one believes oneself to be. But while the howling of any dog may herald some evil time, the appearance of the notorious 'Black Dog' can strike fear and apprehension into the bravest heart.

There seems to be fairly widespread agreement as to what the Black Dog looks like. It is said to be about the size of a small calf, with a long, shaggy black coat and eyes like 'coals of fire'. One of the earliest reports of the Black Dog apparition was recorded in France in AD 856 in the Annales Francorum Regum Bertin. The reports stated that during Mass in a small village church a Black Dog suddenly appeared with flaming red eyes, and this creature ran up into the sanctuary before disappearing. One Irish description of the creature, in Lady Gregory's *Visions and Beliefs* (volume 2), says:

My father told me that one night he was crossing the road, and he turned to the wall to close his shoe. And when he turned again there was something running through the field that was the size of a yearling calf, and black, and it ran across the road, and there was like the sounds of chains in it. And when it came to that rock with the bush on it, it stopped and he could see a red light in its mouth.

And another nineteenth-century description reported by Lady Gregory comes from Kinvara, Co Cork:

> As to the dog that used to be in the road, a friend of his own was driving Father Boyle from Kinvara late one night and there it was—first on the right side and then on the left side of the [horse-drawn] car. At last he told Father Boyle, and he said, 'Look out now for it, and you'll see it no more.' And no more he did, and that was the last of it.

Obviously the good priest's ministrations were effective!

One account of the Black Dog was given to me in the late 1950s by a police sergeant stationed near Derrygonnelly, Co Fermanagh. This particular one was said to haunt a cross-roads outside the village. One evening the sergeant was cycling along the road when to his astonishment a large black dog began to keep pace with his bicycle. It appeared to have no difficulty keeping up, even when he put on a burst of speed. The sergeant said that it 'glided' rather than loped along, and its eyes were large and glittering. 'It filled me with a terrible dread,' he said. On his entering the village street the dog vanished and he, much relieved, rode on to the barracks. He told one or two of his comrades about his adventure and they evinced little surprise, although all were in agreement that 'no good would come of it'. A week later the sergeant fell from a ladder and fractured his leg.

The idea that the Black Dog, called variously in Britain 'Black Shuck', 'Padfoot', 'Thrash', and 'Striker', is a harbinger of evil, if not death, is widespread, and to strike out at the creature is to invite instant reprisal. Yet it has been seen to act as a guardian too, and the person it appoints itself to guard suffers no ill effect. Certainly the behaviour of this manifestation cannot be taken for granted.

In 1928 in Co Derry a student fishing in a local river was unnerved to see a very large black dog loping towards him. Being, like most of us, a coward, the young man abandoned his fishing and with some celerity shinned up a nearby tree. As the dog passed by underneath it lifted its head and snarled

[109]

at the young fisherman, but to his relief it seemed to have other things on its mind. The student recollected that the dog's eyes were 'fiery red'. Happily the young man came to no harm.

A more recent report came from outside Downpatrick, Co Down, and on this occasion the dog appeared to be guarding an old bridge over the River Quoile. Its 'patrol' seemed limited to a small stretch of road on each side. This appears to be a fairly traditional stance; stretches of road, ancient landmarks, crossroads and holy wells all seem to share this manifestation, and the emphasis seems to be on 'guardianship'. Waterways too seem to play a part, as in two of the Irish cases quoted, and there have been similar reports from the vicinity of the pontoon bridge at Pontoon, Co Mayo.

Janet and Colin Bord, two well-known investigators of the paranormal, have suggested that the 'Black Dog' phenomenon is in some way connected to ley lines or ancient trackways and that they are, in a paranormal sense, set to guard the way. This is a very interesting theory and would explain many sightings of this fearsome creature that do take place in or near ancient sites or old roads and tracks.

There are one or two rarer accounts of the Black Dog inside a dwelling. One such account came from a small girl in Co Tyrone who, at the turn of the century, had the experience of seeing a Black Dog in the bedroom in which she had been put to sleep.

> I remember it as clearly as if it had only happened last night. I thought I woke and saw a huge, curly black dog standing in the room, looking at me. Then he came over to the bed with his mouth open, and his great red tongue hanging out. He snuffed at me and licked my hands and face: after which I saw him no more.

Many years later the same little girl, now a grown woman, mentioned the experience to her cousin, and he told her that he had shared the same experience in the self-same room, and that his sister too could vouch for the manifestation.

In many instances of animal manifestation it is not seeing the creature that is commented upon but the hearing of some auditory phenomenon. Horses' hooves, either of a single animal or in twos or fours, seem to be among the most common, as in the case of the farmer's son who heard several horses passing him in a line in Co Fermanagh. In another case at Inchy, near Gort, Co Galway, a young farmer heard what he took to be the sound of deer:

> ... and he heard something come running from Inchy Weir and he could see nothing, but the sound of its feet on the ground was like the sound of a deer. And when it passed by him the dog got between him and the wall and scratched at him, but still he could see nothing but only heard the sound of hooves ...

The fact that other animals may see or hear paranormal manifestations is well documented and, as in the belief that they 'see' the Angel of Death, there are many accounts of animals behaving as though they saw something invisible to their human companions. One man commented on this as he walked near Kiltartan Chapel:

> The dog I had with me ran out into the middle of the road, and there he began to yelp and to fight. I stood and watched him for a while, and surely he was fighting with another dog, but there was nothing to be seen.

And in approximately the same location the same witness said:

> I heard horses galloping past me, I could hear their hooves, and they shod, on the stones of the road. But though I stood aside and looked—it was bright moonlight—there were no horses to be seen.

In the 1960s an owner of one of Ulster's large stately homes told me that sometimes the dogs, a labrador and a retriever, would go through the motions of greeting someone or something coming down the stairs, and from the way they played about and wagged their tails it seemed fairly obvious that they knew who or what they were greeting.

In my own experience of animals seeing what we do not, I can only cite the case of my two Siamese cats after the death of an older cat, who had made up an inseparable threesome. Sorley Boy had died at the age of 15 and been buried under his favourite bush in the garden. For several days his brothers hunted for him, crying and showing every evidence of grief.

Then on the fifth evening they were sitting before the fire consoling one another. Sorley Boy had been in the habit of sitting on a bookshelf beside the chimney-breast, much in the manner of an animated book-end, and it was a vantage-point from which he could keep his eye on all that was going on. To my knowledge neither of the other cats ever sat in 'his' place.

Suddenly Bran stopped washing himself and jumped onto the arm of the chair beside the bookshelf. He stared long and intently into the vacant corner, and then slowly, tentatively stretched out a paw towards the empty space. Finbarr, who was sitting on the rug, watched all this with close attention but he made no attempt to move. Then Bran relaxed, he gave a 'prrr!' and jumped down from the chair as though satisfied with what he had witnessed; and for the rest of the evening neither cat paid the slightest attention to the bookshelf. From where I had witnessed events it did appear that Bran had seen someone or something in the corner of the bookshelf; he had got up on the chair to investigate and then, satisfied that there was nothing amiss and that whoever was there had a right to be there, paid no further heed and resumed his normal station on the rug. Finbarr, who was by nature a nervous cat, showed no fear or apprehension but rather a mild curiosity at whatever was attracting attention in the corner. I did investigate the shelf some minutes later to see if anything could be seen that might have attracted the cat's attention, but I could find nothing.

Some years later, when Bran had already joined Sorley Boy in sleep in the garden, I came into the sitting-room the day after we had buried Finbarr and I saw a grey shape jump down from the arm of my chair, which had been his favourite roost, and head for the fireside rug. My husband was to have a similar experience one evening shortly after this. About twelve months after Finbarr's death a medium friend of mine who had just returned from Australia and was paying us a flying visit remarked: 'There's your little cat whisking round the corner.' At this time she didn't know that Finbarr had died, but realised this only as she 'saw' him in the room. As one of the great legion of cat lovers who have shared their lives with a series of irreplaceable felines, I feel the house that little bit less empty because it seems their happy presences are still about.

The experience that I had was to be echoed by Maureen
Tattershall of Belfast, who wrote to tell me in 1985 about
her small phantom. She had moved into her present home
some ten years earlier, a solid semi-detached house built in
the early 1900s. Almost at once Maureen realised that, along
with the house, she had acquired a 'ghost cat'. She wrote:

> It seemed to be a small grey one, possibly a tabby. It
> appears without warning, often whisking round a door
> or looking down a staircase. It is seen more often during
> the winter months and particularly at Christmas. One
> Christmas we were entertaining a friend of my daughter's
> who knew nothing of our shadowy resident. During the
> evening she went into the hall to make a telephone call.
> As she opened the door from the front room, the cat
> dashed past her—and promptly vanished. She saw it quite
> distinctly.

Maureen went on to explain that everyone in the family seemed
to have seen it at some time; on one occasion her daughter
was standing with her at the front door and the little grey cat
hopped over their feet! Her own cats seemed to take the little
visitor for granted, but occasionally they acknowledged its
presence:

> I sometimes watched one of them lift a head, follow
> something with the eye—something that seems to be
> moving across the room—then settle down to sleep again.
> Oddly, when our cats see the ghost one, I don't see it at
> the same time.

A delightful phantom, and one that, as Maureen Tattershall
observed, 'must have been very attached to the house in its
lifetime'.

In the *Proceedings of the Society for Psychical Research*
(volume 41, 1922-23), a similar happening in 1884 is reported
by a mother and daughter, Mrs Greifenberg and Mrs Erni
Greifenberg, during their midday lunch. They saw a white
Angora cat with green eyes under the table. The cat marched
round the table, and went noiselessly out of the door and
half-way down the passage, turned and stared at the two
women, then dissolved away under the gaze. The same appari-

tional cat went through the same performance a year later, in Leipzig. This apparition then was not attached to a particular place, but rather to people, which is quite unusual.

In 1923 another correspondent wrote to the SPR that in July 1909 her sister's cat, Smokey, a pure-bred blue Persian, who had been ill and had later died, appeared in the garden close to where she had been buried the previous June. Miss Green writes:

> My sister and I were at breakfast and I was reading a letter aloud to her . . . Suddenly I saw her look absolutely scared and gazing out of the window. I said, 'What is the matter?', and she said, 'There's Smokey walking across the grass.' We both rushed to the window and saw Smokey, looking very ill, her coat rough and staring, and walking lamely across the grass in front of the window, three or four yards from it . . .

The writer said that the cat ignored their calls, and then her sister ran into the garden, but lost sight of it. It subsequently reappeared and was seen by a servant in the house. All in all four people attested that they saw Smokey on that occasion, and the cat did not appear again. The witness insisted that she had never before seen anything 'supernormal' but that her sister, the owner of the cat, did appear to possess ESP. She wondered if as a result of this her sister could have conveyed her 'sight' of the cat telepathically to other percipients.

On reading this case one has to take into account the possibility that where a much-loved pet is concerned, there is a possibility of 'wishful thinking' or some hallucinatory event that stems from grief. In the case of Maureen Tattershall, and indeed the two German women who did not appear to have a connection with the phantom cat in Leipzig, this possibility can be ruled out. In my own case, while I grieved over the deaths of my own Siamese cats in their old age it was not unexpected, and so I was sad but not distraught, as I might have been in more harrowing circumstances. In the case of Miss Green one supposes that her feelings over Smokey would have been akin to mine, and while she may have been influenced by her sister's more obvious grief and ESP ability, it doesn't explain how the same cat was seen by a friend visiting the house, and by the maid, whose emotional involvement in the cat's illness and death was probably minimal. So if one rules out 'wishful thinking' then one has to look at other possibilities, including some form of telepathic transmission of the apparition. But then, cats are such mysterious creatures one is scarcely surprised if they defy convention and continue to go about their business in their own peculiar fashion!

Not that cats are the only pets to manifest. Dogs too have this facility on occasion. An acquaintance of mine who lived for some years at Invermore House in Co Antrim heard one of her terriers, recently deceased, snuffling about the room for some time as if exploring, in his own inimitable way, some promising mousehole!

A priest friend too, a Father V., once rang me from Athlone to tell me that the house he was staying in had a phantom dog. The dog would manifest itself by pushing open the bedroom door, trotting up to the bed, then jumping up. After turning round two or three times the invisible canine would settle for a sleep beside Father V.'s reluctant toes. It was a ritual that never varied, then after a few minutes the sense of weight on the bedclothes would gradually disappear. As my clerical friend was a somewhat explosive mixture of Irish and Italian, I had to allow him to pause to draw breath in the telling of the tale before suggesting that he should make tentative enquiries of the household about a previous 'dog incumbent' of the front bedroom.

Some nights later Father V. rang me again to say that, having taken my advice, he had learned that the previous owner of the house, an elderly unmarried woman, had owned a small dog that had been a great pet. The dog had in fact predeceased his owner after an unfortunate confrontation with a milk lorry. The front room had been the one occupied by the woman in her lifetime, and the dog had been in the habit of keeping her company. Oddly enough, once Father V. had made this discovery the visitations stopped, and perversely my friend then missed his nightly visitor. 'I said a prayer for the wee man and his mistress,' he told me. 'Our Lord, I'm sure, has a place for our little friend.' A sentiment akin to my own!

The sensitivity of animals brought into contact with the

paranormal is well known, although their actual reactions may differ. Dogs, for example, brought to alleged 'haunted areas' may well exhibit fear, aggression and, on occasion, paralytic terror. Cats on the other hand may hiss and spit but are more inclined to take up a 'watchful' stance, and will also exhibit curiosity.

A schoolteacher in Co Fermanagh, Kevin McNally, told me of a very curious incident that took place in the 1940s involving a greyhound. One evening Kevin heard the dog scratching and whining at the kitchen door to be let in, and on opening it he found the dog in a state of abject terror. Earlier that evening his elderly father had set out with the dog for a walk across the fields; now the dog had come home alone, and his father was nowhere to be seen. Fearing that some accident might have befallen his father, Kevin set off down the lane at the trot, only to meet his father in a somewhat agitated state of mind hurrying towards him.

What had happened was this. The father had taken the dog across the fields towards the old family home, now derelict. As they headed for a gap in the hedge coming up to the house, Kevin's father saw, approaching the gap from the direction of the house, an elderly woman dressed in black. As it appeared obvious that they would reach the narrow gap at about the same time, the father stood to one side to let her come through, at the same time bidding her good evening. But just as she reached the gap, to his consternation, she simply vanished. At once the greyhound, normally a friendly and placid animal, gave a great yelp, and tore the lead from the old man's hand and fled. Kevin took up the story: 'I can verify that when the dog arrived back here he was in an awful state, trembling and whimpering. He couldn't be persuaded out of the house for nearly a day.'

Another incident, which took place in Co Kilkenny, concerns canine reactions of a different kind. The witness reported that he was crossing a bridge with his dog, a small terrier, when all at once the dog began to bark and yelp in a vicious manner, his attention rooted to 'something' on the side of the road. At first the witness saw nothing; then what he took to be a grey shape vanished into the ditch. As soon as this happened the dog's behaviour became normal again. The witness could find nothing in the ditch, and seemed certain that it was not another creature, simply a 'shape'. Local enquiry by the witness revealed that horses frequently had to be coaxed past that particular spot, and older inhabitants said a man had been killed there. Now such tales abound in the countryside, and one should treat them with a certain amount of caution; nevertheless the witness, a local farmer not normally given to 'vapours', stuck to the tale, and so eventually it was told to me.

Rosamond, Lady Langham, of Tempo Manor in Co Fermanagh also told me of how during the disturbances in the house that occurred after the skull of the boy was brought inside (see chapter 6) the family dogs also refused to enter the passage leading to the private museum or the room itself. For such courageous little dogs to exhibit fear inside their own home must surely have indicated that something basic was amiss.

So far this chapter has dealt with animal sensitivity and the apparitions of animals, but a rarer paranormal manifestation is that which takes place when a material animal takes upon itself to be the harbinger of evil tidings, and in this category Ireland must surely possess one of the rarest examples of this, in the shape of the Gormanston Foxes.

The tradition of the Gormanston Foxes goes back to early times. The Preston family with whom they are associated were not of Celtic origin but came from Lancashire. In 1361 Sir Robert de Preston set sail for Ireland and settled at Gormanston, Co Meath, a lovely manorial dwelling by the sea. It was his great-grandson who became the first Viscount Gormanston. Yet for all that, there were a dozen viscounts before the story of the foxes was set down in the time of the Thirteenth Viscount in 1876. His wife, Lucretia, had of course heard of the tradition that before the death of the lord of Gormanston the foxes would keep vigil at the castle; but she had dismissed this tale with a smile.

Then her husband fell seriously ill, and a few days before his death Lord Gormanston at his own request was brought down into the library, where he might sit in a chair and look out over the demesne. Lady Lucretia kept him company, and as she sat in the window she saw a number of foxes sitting on the grass on the far side of the gravel drive, but close to and in full view of the castle windows. She was naturally very up-set, and sent her two sons and some servants to drive them away, but the foxes appeared to have lost all fear of humans and when chased simply retreated to the shrubbery, only to take up their stations once more as soon as the men retreated indoors. That night Lord Gormanston suffered a relapse and died. As his funeral procession left the castle for the church-yard, his daughter, the Hon Mrs John Farrell, saw a number of foxes loping across the fields and following the cortège.

One of those young men who had taken a stick to the foxes on that occasion was to succeed his father, as Jenico, Four-teenth Viscount Gormanston. He died in 1907 in his seventieth year in a private nursing home in Dublin. The remains were taken by road to the family chapel at Gormanston. The funeral was due to take place the next day, when the viscount would be laid to rest in the family vault. On this sad occasion it was his second son, Colonel the Hon Richard Preston DSO, who undertook to keep vigil with his father's body in the chapel overnight; and this is his account, as related in the *Franciscan College Annual*, 1964:

> Some time around midnight, or in the very early hours of the morning, I became aware of the sound of snuffling and whining at the door of the chapel at the west end, that is, the door opposite the altar. My elder brother at that time was breeding Irish wolfhounds and had a litter of puppies. Thinking the yard gate had been left open by mistake and that the puppies had got out, I went and opened the chapel door . . .

What Colonel Preston saw must have unnerved him consider-ably, for in the light of the candles about the coffin he saw outside the door at least four or five foxes, simply sitting and staring into the chapel. They showed no fear of him at all. Considerably alarmed, Colonel Preston tried a side door, but there too were several foxes, lying down or simply sitting in an attitude of watchfulness. Colonel Preston continued:

> I instinctively aimed a kick at the nearest one, but he merely avoided my foot and sat down again a yard or two away. I remained in the chapel until shortly before

daylight, when the noise of the whining and snuffling ceased, and on going out I found that the foxes had made off.

Local hunt enthusiasts knew that to try to have any sport if the lord of the castle lay on his deathbed was out of the question. One elderly hunt follower told a visitor: 'You'll get no sport, sir, the foxes are all away to the old lord's dying.'

It is interesting to note that the arms of the Viscounts Gormanston show two foxes, one as a supporter of the shield and one as the crest. It is said that the reason for the foxes' vigil is that an earlier Lord Gormanston showed compassion towards a pregnant vixen, and ever after the foxes came to support the Prestons in their hour of grief.

Gormanston Castle is now Gormanston College, and in the hands of the order of Saint Francis. With such a patron, the foxes of Gormanston may rest content.

Matters Miscellaneous

In the course of some twenty-five years of research into the paranormal, there are bound to be particular events that stick in one's mind or an account that has a curiously original twist to it. In this concluding chapter I crave the reader's indulgence for looking at one or two tales, both ancient and modern, that have stayed in my mind over the years.

Ireland is full of legends and tales about the realm of the faerie and the paranormal. As is the case in other Celtic communities, sometimes it can be difficult to disentangle fact from folk tradition. This first account, however, has quite a respectable historical background and concerns an apparition and a lawsuit. The reason for my particular interest is that I live only two or three miles from the grave of the man concerned in the account.

My interest was aroused one afternoon when an Anglican rector of my acquaintance asked me if I had seen the 'crooked gravestone' belonging to James Haddock in the grounds of Drumbeg Church. He told me that, according to local tradition, the flat stone covering James Haddock's last resting-place never lay straight, no matter how often attempts were made to rectify it.

Our story begins in the year 1662 in the vicinity of Drumbeg, Co Down, then called Drumbridge. It was a late autumn evening when Francis Taverner or Toweny, porter and servant to Lord Chichester, was riding homewards from Hillsborough, Co Down, to Mallon, Co Antrim. Mallon, now Malone, is on the outskirts of what has now become greater Belfast.

Suddenly there appeared beside him an apparition clad in a long white robe and on horseback, and in company with two other riders. The apparition bore a resemblance to one James Haddock, who had been known to Taverner and whose remains now lay in the churchyard at Drumbeg. It is believed that Haddock had died somewhere about 1657. When the terrified Taverner asked what in God's name he required and who he was, the apparition identified itself by recalling a trivial incident at which they had both been present in the house of Francis Taverner's father. The apparition seemed greatly agitated, and begged Taverner to ride with it, as it had a request to make of him.

Understandably Taverner declined the 'honour', and spurring his horse, which was also exhibiting extreme alarm, he left the apparition behind at the crossroads amid a sound 'like a mighty wind' and with other noises that would have been guaranteed to frighten a lesser man out of his senses. Unfortunately, if Taverner assumed that he had heard the last of Haddock's pleas for help he was to be sadly disillusioned. The following night the apparition appeared to Taverner at his own fireside, amid noises and sounds of music, and again begged leave to tell its disconcerted host what errand it wished Taverner to undertake on its behalf.

The nub of the matter was a story of domestic malpractice. Haddock explained that his widow, Eleanor Walsh or Welsh, had married again, to a man called Davis. Davis had been known to Haddock in life, and he had made him one of the executors of his will. Now Davis had abused this trust and had seen fit to misappropriate certain property bequeathed to Haddock's young son, David, and so Haddock wished Francis Taverner to bring the abuse to the notice of the authorities.

Despite the pleadings of the distracted apparition, Taverner was loath to involve himself in the affairs of his neighbours, particularly as Davis was known to be a violent man. Understandably too he saw no good reason why anyone should believe his bizarre tale, and he stood a very good chance of being accused of witchcraft or of being locked up as a lunatic. So again he protested that he could not help.

The angry apparition then warned him that it would 'give him no peace', and proceeded to carry out that threat by appearing nightly accompanied by diverse thuds and bangs and sometimes by music, which sounded as though it had been played on a flute. Every waking moment of the unfortunate Taverner was fraught with unease. Then one night he woke to find the apparition bending over him and demanding with the utmost menace that the message be delivered to Eleanor Walsh. To reinforce the argument, Haddock's ghost then threatened to 'tear Taverner to pieces', a threat that his victim felt it was quite capable of carrying out.

Hoping that a change of venue might deter his unearthly visitor, Francis Taverner took himself off to stay with friends in Belfast, but alas the apparition followed him there, where it was seen by others and, to reinforce the idea of paranormal vengeance, indulged in some 'shape shifting' before vanishing with a clap of thunder.

Finally, 'in extremis', Taverner confided the sequence of events to the family of his master, Lord Chichester, whose chaplain, a Mr James South, advised him to do as the apparition desired and carry a message to Eleanor Walsh. For some days after doing this Taverner was not troubled by any visitation. Then Haddock appeared again, and this time demanded that the same message be carried to the executors of the will.

In that connection there was a distinct problem, as Davis would then know that Taverner was interfering in his affairs. When the affrighted Taverner asked the apparition if Davis would do him hurt he received a very evasive reply, but it did promise that it would threaten Davis and 'put the fear of God into him'. With that Taverner had to be content. Having completed the preliminaries, he laid the case before the Church Court of the famous Bishop Jeremy Taylor, whose diocese was Down.

The worthy bishop, it has to be said, was less interested in Taverner's original mission than in the prospect of eliciting some spiritual information from the apparition, through Taverner. He bade Taverner question the spirit about the world beyond. He told him to ask questions such as 'Whence came you?', 'Where is your abode?' and 'Are you a good spirit?'—all of which one feels was less than helpful to poor Francis Taverner.

That night, after his encounter with the bishop, Francis Taverner was in the house of Lord Conway, where he had some business to transact for his master. This time the apparition manifested itself in the courtyard of the house: according to reports it 'crawled over the wall'. It did give Taverner the welcome news that it would trouble him no more, but warned that the executors must keep their word or it would do them ill. Among other things, Haddock's ghost had promised certain signs and wonders, and among these were that his gravestone would lie crooked, one assumes as a symbol of 'crooked dealings'. That part can be seen to be true, and as far as I know the situation continues to this day.

On the matter of the bishop's questions, Taverner received little response. The apparition gave no definite answers but vanished in a flash of white over the wall, to the sound of music—'a most melodious twang', as the account relates.

So the action to investigate the executors was brought to the Bishop's Court at Carrickfergus, Co Antrim. The counsel for Davis and the other executor, a man called John Costlett, the young boy's uncle, was all set to have some sport with the unhappy Taverner—a fact that Taverner was all too gloomily aware of, having been elected to speak on behalf of a discarnate being.

It is said that after a few pithy remarks, when the counsel for the defence asked Taverner if he had any witness he might care to call, Taverner in desperation cried, 'Call James Haddock.' Naturally the court-room began to guffaw and make very pointed remarks about Taverner's sanity.

Bishop Taylor, however, having come this far was determined to see the bizarre case through to the end. He ordered the court usher to do as Taverner desired. Three times the usher cried out in a loud voice, 'Call James Haddock,' and on the third cry a clap of thunder rent the air and a hand was seen on the witness table, while a voice declared, 'Is that enough?' It most certainly was for the hushed court-room and for Bishop Taylor, who promptly ordered a thorough investigation into the affairs of young David Haddock. Justice in fact had been seen to be done, as the guilty parties, Davis and Costlett, were only too well aware.

It is said that Davis set out from the court in a terrible rage, and things might have gone ill for Francis Taverner had not a curious accident occurred. On the Drumbridge road Davis's horse started with fright at 'something', and Davis was thrown and broke his neck. Five years later the other executor, John Costlett, who had once more begun to harass his young nephew, was also killed by a fall from his horse, and so Haddock's revenge was complete.

So it came to pass that a dead man gave evidence in a court of law, and won his case. However bizarre we may find this account, the interesting thing is that it does appear to have its basis in historical fact. The secretary to the bishop at that time was a Mr Thomas Alcock, who set it down in a letter, and in the main the details are the same as were reported at the time by Francis Taverner. There are minor variants, of course. One report says that the apparition was not on horseback but stood in the road before Taverner, and then climbed up behind him, smelling most dolefully of decay. There are conflicting reports about how many people saw the apparition or heard the ghostly music; but in general the story remains the same, and an account was published in *Saducismus Triumphatus* by Joseph Glanvill FRS, chaplain in ordinary to King Charles II.

As far as I am concerned there is a postscript. In autumn 1973 I received an anonymous but very agitated telephone call from an elderly woman. She had that rare quality, an ability to convey information clearly and succinctly. She told me that she had driven down in her car to post a letter in a letter-box that is let into the wall of Drumbeg church. As she was standing beside the wall she saw in the gathering twilight a man's head bobbing up and down along the inside of the wall. 'It was as though he was on a trotting horse,' she said. She was alarmed that the head appeared to have no features, and as he approached her she flung dignity to the winds and ran for the car. The only other information she gave me was that the head seemed to be above a tall collar, and that the 'bobbing' motion was quite rhythmic. She was also familiar with the tale of Haddock's ghost, for she asked me if I thought that was whom she had seen.

She was not prepared to give me her name, but I have no reason to doubt her account. The walls of the churchyard would follow very roughly an old roadway from Drumbridge to Mallon, and it would have been somewhere close to the church that Francis Taverner had his memorable encounter with the ghost of James Haddock over two centuries ago.

One paranormal theory that has always interested me is the idea that stone has the capacity to retain images and sounds from the past. Stone building evoke in most people a sense of permanence and continuity, and perhaps the reason for this is that as sentient beings we recognise the internal quality of the fabric of such places, the 'spirit of the stone' if you like. On numerous occasions the paranormal has manifested itself in connection with stone circles, stone tombs, castles, amphitheatres, and the like. The churchyard wall of Drumbeg is of stone, and some of the stone used in the building of it may conceivably bear the imprint of what happened along that particular stretch of road.

Another small stone edifice in Co Down may have haunting echoes of its own. It is a small stone bridge on the Strangford Road, called locally Fiddler's Bridge. This bridge in the mid-nineteenth century was alleged to be the mute witness of the particularly unpleasant murder of a travelling musician. This man earned his living by going about with his fiddle and playing at wakes and weddings and for the amusement of the customers in the local taverns. It was one of the latter venues that was to prove the unfortunate man's undoing. One evening as a group of workmen downed their pints in Raholp Inn, the fiddler did his best to entertain them, but when called upon to play a certain tune with strong political overtones, the man quietly but resolutely refused. Angered at his refusal and by now well 'in their cups', the men set upon him and beat him to death.

Once the horrid deed was done the men sobered up considerably, and in fear of the summary justice that they knew would follow once it was discovered, they now set about hiding the fiddler's remains. So they carried the corpse along the Scraw Pad, a small trackway that led round the village and onto the very stretch of road they were engaged in building between Downpatrick and Strangford. There they laid the fiddler in a shallow grave.

The following few days brought torrential rain, and little work was done on the road, but when the guilty crew assembled for work on the next fair morning they found that the rain had worked the soil from the grave, and part of the body was now on view. A second attempt at 'burying the evidence' was made; and as there is no record of a conviction for the crime, it would appear that their plotting was successful. As

the grave itself has never been found—although by tradition
the Fiddler's Bridge marks the spot—one can only conclude
that the basis of this story may derive from some deathbed
confession.

Within sight of this little stone bridge, local people have
seen lights hovering about, not unlike the rough torchlights
of long ago. While I have yet to discover anyone who has seen
the lights for themselves, it is in the oral tradition of the area.
I did wonder too, as the bridge is made of stone, had some
'imprinting' of that dreadful night's deed taken place, especially
with its close affinity to water, which does tend to deepen the
extrasensory experience?

Other roads in the vicinity of Downpatrick have their share
of hauntings. The stretch of road known as the Finnebrogue
Straight is said to be haunted by an old woman in a shawl,
and by a phantom stage-coach. The main Killyleagh-to-Down-
patrick Road is haunted by the apparitions of two children
near Three Mile Hill; but then, old roads and ancient tracks
have had a peculiar way of recording their travellers from
time immemorial.

Nearby stand the haunted gates of Finnebrogue, which once
marked the entrance to Finnebrogue House not far from Inch
Abbey, Co Down. All that the stranger will see nowadays,
enclosed behind a stout stone wall, are two crumbling stone
pillars, the entrance having been moved a short distance down
the road. Legend has it that the pillars were built with stone
taken from the ruined abbey, and that from the moment the
gates were hung on the pillars, things began to go very wrong
indeed. For one thing the gates refused to stay put: they were
found time and time again lying on the ground, despite strenu-
ous efforts to hang them. Even with guards posted to see what
vandals were causing such a 'hullabaloo' it was no use; for
under the eyes of the watchers the gates simply detached themselves from their hinges and crashed to the ground. Horses
were afraid to venture through the gates, and men were
forced to dismount and lead their frightened animals through,
or abandon them altogether. Eventually the gates were removed
and the pillars abandoned to whatever power had command
over them, and so they have remained to this day.

In Holywood, Co Down, which, as its name implies, was

once the seat of much religious life and learning, and now a small but thriving town on the road between Belfast and the seaside resort of Bangor, there is a ghostly tale that concerns not an abbey but Chiccarino's, a pub and licensed restaurant. The ghost in this case specialised in 'after-hours' visitations. Upon arrival one morning the then owner found the back door firmly jammed by a heavy carton of stationery, which appeared to have been thrown down the stairs from the upper store-rooms. On another occasion it was a beer crate, and lights too were switched on after the owners had locked up for the night. The wife of the owner, Barbara Bradley, also sensed a 'presence' in the pub, but never saw anything. A more prosaic disturbance was the flushing of the toilets after the place was closed and the owners knew themselves to be the only people on the premises. 'That happened all the time,' said Barbara, 'and when my husband investigated, the place was empty and the cistern filling.' Modesty, she pointed out, had prevented her from carrying out an investigation! It is interesting to note that the customers had no paranormal experiences: it all seemed to happen after hours and either to the owners or the staff. Obviously a thoughtful entity was at work here, who was not disposed to frighten off the customers!

Another pub, near Omagh, Co Tyrone, was haunted by a young man in a brown suit, who appeared in the bar itself from time to time. My informant, Mr Hugh Donnelly, told me that there had been a road accident outside the pub some time before, and a man was killed. Whether one could make a connection is obviously open to query. Mr Donnelly also told me of an experience he had had on the road past 'Rosses Planting', near Ballygawley, Co Tyrone. One morning at about 1.30 a.m. Mr Donnelly was cycling along the road when he heard a noise and saw in front of him a large white pig, which seemed to match its pace to his. It finally vanished at a spot where the road went over water. What surprises me is that apparitional pigs seem to engender far more horror than their canine counterparts!

One house that appeared to have quite a variety of disturbances, and so remains very clearly in my mind, was Invermore House at Larne, Co Antrim. An early nineteenth-century building, it has now passed from private ownership and its demesne has become a housing development: such is the march of progress. At the time I was privileged to visit it some of its former glory still clung to its venerable walls and sunlit garden. I was invited by the owner, Miss Heather McClane, who, with two friends, the Misses Thompson, lived in the house with a small and attractive collection of canine companions. One reason too why I remember the Invermore case is that the witnesses, while quite anxious about events, were all so charming, helpful and painstaking in their descriptions; they made the life of this researcher so much more agreeable.

The original house, so Miss McClane told me, had been built in the early 1800s, while extensive additions had been built about 1846. The owners before her had been Howdens and Fishers, and the original dwelling had been the property of the Casement family of Co Antrim. Several memorials to these families are to be found in local graveyards including that of Saint Cedma's churchyard. A stained-glass window in Gondemore church commemorates the Howdens.

In a telephone call in the summer of 1981 Miss Thompson asked me to come and see them if I could, as they were somewhat worried about events in the house. Even that telephone call was to be relevant, as Miss Thompson told me that while we were talking she had heard the front door close, and presumed that her sister, Anne, had just come in. A trivial incident, but one that I was to remember later. About a week after that telephone call I drove to Larne with my husband, who was to act as witness and operate the tape recorder. The brief account of some of the 'goings-on' had attracted my interest, especially as it seemed likely that at least two of the women had heard the banshee, and as there had been a number of manifestations of some intensity in the house. As it turned out, another witness was present when we got there, a Mr McConkey, who helped out from time to time with some of the jobs around the place and in general acted as adviser and friend to the ladies.

As we sat in that elegant nineteenth-century drawing-room, looking out over the garden one had a glimpse of what the house must have been like in its heyday. Now the town pressed in upon it, and the soaring costs of keeping up such a large dwelling would eventually be its ruination. Miss McClane, who had some knowledge of the history of the house, told me how a century before funeral urns had been discovered in the garden, with human remains still in them. The house was said locally to be 'haunted', but outside of what they had experienced themselves she had come across no specific tales of hauntings. As it transpired, the experiences of the occupants of Invermore were quite enough to be going on with!

Firstly there was the apparition of a previous owner, a Miss (Mrs?) Fisher, which had been seen in the hall by Miss McClane. She described her as a small woman, 'quite ordinary', and she seemed solid and real. She had seen her once in the drawing-room too. The other apparition seen by Miss McClane was neither small nor ordinary, but quite the reverse! This sighting happened one night as Miss McClane was coming from her bedroom to the bathroom on the upper floor of the house. The apparition was that of a man, whom she described graphically as 'the Sandeman Port man', that is, a man clad in a flowing cloak with a hat on his head. He had a small neatly trimmed beard and saturnine features. She first saw him standing quite motionless in the corridor in the dim light, but on her return from the bathroom, to Miss McClane's astonishment, he was still there, and she had to pass him a second time. It was only when she reached the sanctuary of her bedroom that she found she was trembling with fright.

After a discussion we arrived at the suggestion that he was or could have been a nineteenth-century gentleman in evening or at least outdoor clothes, or perhaps from a little later, in the early part of this century. Miss McClane remarked that he reminded her of Sir Roger Casement, who was hanged in 1916 for his activities in preparation for the Easter Rising. The Casement family had certainly occupied the house, and it was believed that Sir Roger had been a visitor to it, if not a permanent resident. She felt that the apparition had 'seen' her and that some kind of recognition passed between them. As to the time during which he was in view as a 'solid' manifestation, she reckoned it would have been about a minute or two as she went from one room to the other. This apparition was only seen on the one occasion.

Then there was 'the whispering'. This emanated from a point outside the room known as the Green Room, on the upper floor, not far from the head of the stairs. 'It was as though two women were having a conversation, low enough for the sound to carry but not clear enough for their words to be distinguished'—that was the way one witness put it. Mr McConkey heard this manifestation as he came into the hall one afternoon through the front door. He thought that the ladies of the house were in, and when he got no reply to his words of greeting he went upstairs and found no-one about. He had had several experiences in the Blue Bedroom that tallied with the feelings of the rest of the household, who told me quite unequivocally that they would not sleep in the room. When pressed, the ladies said that there was a 'funny feeling' about it and that it felt cold and unwelcoming, a coldness they felt was not entirely explicable. The Blue Room was one of the rooms in the oldest part of the house, an odd, smallish chamber reached by a short flight of steps, and there was a general consensus that it had been a child's room—although there were no special features to indicate this.

Mr McConkey was the only one who had actually slept in it, and he told of the sensation of acute cold that seemed to affect the right-hand side of the bed. He said that he had woken on more than one occasion to find the right side of his body frozen, as though it had been in a freezer, and yet the left side of his body was at quite a normal temperature. When asked if he felt that the 'cold' came from any particular direction, he said that it seemed to have some connection with the area where the dressing-table stood, and while this was situated at the farthest spot from both door and window, he was quite firm in his belief that the 'cold spot' was there.

On another night, shortly after he had got into bed, the whole bed began to vibrate, slowly at first and then faster and faster until even the headboard was shaking. This too was accompanied by a drop in temperature. Despite these unpleasant experiences Mr McConkey continued to sleep there and said very prosaically that they didn't annoy him, and that in any case, knowing something of the room's reputation, he had been expecting something to happen!

I paid a visit to the Blue Room and found it to be just as it had been described and with a distinctly unwelcome atmosphere. It was certainly not a room I would have enjoyed sojourning in myself. Mr McConkey accompanied the ladies and myself upstairs, and on entering the room he said he could feel 'a very cold spot'. I stood where he indicated but felt nothing unusual, although there was a general chill about the room, even on that sunny afternoon. The Blue Room was not far from where Miss McClane had seen the apparition of the bearded man.

The Misses Thompson told me that the house was 'full of noises'; all the occupants had heard them from time to time. One was of 'a woman's feet in slippers' crossing the attic floor, from corner to corner. The attics may have been servants' quarters at some time, as the stairs went right up to them. Downstairs, in a room that had once served as a small library or study, Miss Thompson had heard one afternoon when she was in the kitchen the sound of someone 'moving books about'. On investigation she found that a small table had been moved to block the door, and the drawers in it lay open, as though someone had been looking for something in a hurry. This was the only time that furniture was moved, although when the household went to bed the noises from the study were quite loud, with thuds and bangs; and one of the elderly dogs, who sometimes slept in the study in her basket, would bark almost continuously the whole night.

It was then that I heard the sequel to the incident that I mentioned earlier. It seems that as I was having that telephone conversation with Miss Thompson about visiting Invermore, the front door was heard to open and close, and Miss Thompson had broken off the conversation to call, 'Is that you, Anne?' But no-one had come in at all during that time.

Other sounds in the house included that of a small dog sniffing along the back of the wardrobe—this sound was attributed to a late lamented Scottie called Angus—and the more frightening sound of a heavy animal galloping up and down the bedroom corridor, and at times skidding right up to the door.

While I have mentioned the Invermore banshee briefly elsewhere, I feel that this is an appropriate place to go into the account more fully. In the first place neither Miss McClane nor Miss Thompson were certain what they had heard, but they gave me a very succinct description of the two separate occasions when they heard what one may take to be the banshee.

The first time Miss Thompson heard the sound it was coming

from the garden, over by the hedge near the road. She admitted that she could not tell what it was, save that it was a wailing sound that went on and on and finally rose to a shriek. She commented that 'it must have had a massive pair of lungs on it,' as it kept up the howling ad infinitum. This particular attribute, of not having to draw breath, is often noted as a feature of the banshee cry. About twenty-four hours afterwards an aunt died. It is worthy of note that in some parts of Ireland there is a contention that the banshee only wails for the head of the house, or only for a man, but this was not the case at Invermore.

It was after the second 'banshee' incident, however, that they had decided to consult me. Miss Thompson considered that it must have been going on for some time, as she felt that she had been listening to it subconsciously before she woke up. The sounds ranged from this 'roaring' to an eldritch shriek. Remarkably, the two small dogs that kept their mistresses company in the room slept on peacefully through the din. 'Our hair quite literally stood on end,' said Miss McClane, 'and neither of us was keen to get out of bed to investigate.' With all the lights blazing, they waited for the dreadful sound to die away, but it continued for several minutes.

When I questioned them about the sound itself, whether it was 'human-like' or 'animal-like', the women were unsure. Somehow it didn't seem like either, and they agreed that it was like nothing they had ever heard before. Miss Thompson remarked that on the first occasion when she had heard the wailing in the garden it was such a lonely sound that she 'had felt sorry for it'. That was not how she felt the second time, as sheer fright overtook her. The two women had been too upset to leave the bedroom, even to calm their nerves with a cup of tea, and they had spent the rest of the night with the lights on.

In the aftermath of such an experience there were one or two matters to note. Both women insisted that the noise was 'in the room'. This is a most unusual experience, in that the majority of reports of the banshee locate it outside, often under a window or sitting on a window-ledge. No death followed this incident, although they did have a very ill relative in hospital at the time. After further discussion both women felt that although they had no previous experience of such a manifestation, what they had heard was in fact the *bean sí*, Ireland's supernatural death messenger.

Now it was my turn to have a personal demonstration from the unseen occupants of Invermore. On arrival we had left the car outside the main door on the driveway that sloped only gently down to the main gate, some distance from the house. When we said our goodbyes and were escorted out to our car we found that the car, all by itself, had executed a right-angle turn onto the lawns at the side of the house, having to mount a verge in the course of this manoeuvre, and it had come to rest a few yards from a large greenhouse. The car doors were still locked and the hand-brake on. I must confess that I would have given anything to have a photograph of my husband's face as, with the help of Miss McClane and Miss Thompson, we retrieved the errant car and set it back on the driveway!

As this chapter was in a sense an indulgence for me in looking back on one or two of the more memorable events witnessed or told to me over the years, it seems appropriate here to relate one more incident. In the winter of 1986 I was invited to speak to a women's organisation at Downpatrick, Co Down. The group met in a nineteenth-century house in the town, which during its somewhat chequered career had also served as a 'house of correction'. We met in a downstairs room, and the conversation was both lively and convivial. Towards the end of my talk I heard someone moving about in one of the upper rooms, and each time as they retraced their steps they trod on a floor-board that let out an audible squeak of protest. Idly I wondered what other group was meeting upstairs.

At the end of the evening, as I was being escorted across the hall to the door, I asked the chairwoman who it was upstairs. She paled visibly. 'There's no-one here but us,' she said, casting apprehensive glances towards the darkened staircase; 'but the house is supposed to be haunted by a postman: "Old George" they call him.' Plainly, she did not relish in the least the thought of a step on the stair . . .

Appendix A

Stanley Wylie: 'Someone looked out into the hall and said, "Who closed the door?" . . . It was a solid front door, and the door had been wide open and suddenly it was very firmly shut. It took two or three of us to open it, and nobody had come in or out at all . . . We were a little bit shaken by this experience . . .' On disturbances in the cellar: 'We were getting noises from microphones rigged in the cellar. There were a few planks around; just to make sure, we had put flour down and also marked the planks, where they were, so if they moved we would see . . . About 2 a.m. we decided to go down to the cellar, so we went down and looked around . . . We saw that although there were no signs of any footprints at all on the floor, the planks had in actual fact moved position . . .'

Trevor Hanna (journalist): 'Almost all the sounds seemed to be coming from the cellar . . . There were noises like the squawking of a bird, a rumble like a distant motorcycle . . . scraping noises, thuds, and a sound like a latch being lifted. Then there was a rumble from the microphone in the cellar as though it had been moved . . . a metallic rapping . . . and at one stage a tremendous crash, a growling sound, and then another crash . . . I remember one of the party, a very well-built guy, and he could not get that door open. Another member of the party joined him and put his arms around his waist . . . they still could not get the door open; then Sheila came along and put her hand on the door, and the door opened as if it were a perfectly oiled working door.'

Kay Kennedy (a journalist who went up separately some months later in 1961): 'In the room where Billy [the photographer] and myself were [on the ground floor] the door opened . . . The door was about three inches thick, a heavy

[134]

oak door. I got Billy to shut it, and then I looked a few minutes later and it was open again . . . We got a great big boulder between us and pushed it over against the door. We went back and sat down, and the door flew open . . .' This witness also had slates dropped on her from the roof on a night that she maintained was windless and when nothing else was moving.

Sharon Anderson (who visited the site in the 1960s with her brother after the investigation): 'We were walking along and something caught my attention . . . and I saw something forming . . . but thought that it must have been my imagination. So I distinctly remember shaking my head and looking away and then looking back again . . . it was clearer than it was the first time, and I could see that it was a man wearing what I took to be a long white nightshirt, and he had long dark hair . . .'

Mrs Evelyn McAuley (experience in 1937 outside Gillhall gates): 'I was on holiday in Blackskull, near Dromore, with my girl-friend. We were to get the bus . . . As it was a lovely night and the moon was shining brightly we decided to walk along to Gillhall . . . As I was young I didn't know anything about Gillhall, I had never heard of it before. When we got to Gillhall we stood for a few minutes and saw the bus come round the corner. So I looked up the avenue towards Gillhall and then I saw the lady. She wore black, she walked very erectly, and round her face was a small veil . . . Both her hands were together and crossed. I thought that she was on her way to the bus, but she never came . . .'

Danny Johnston (a local man living within a short distance of Gillhall): 'I left my girl-friend off in town, where she lived . . . It was about half twelve or quarter to one in the morning. I was coming home, just driving normally, maybe a hundred yards from Gillhall gates, when this woman came walking straight across the road. You see, there's a laneway just opposite the gates entrance. She never looked left nor right; I braked . . . I turned round to look, I thought maybe she was in a car with someone. She definitely couldn't have got through the gates, and there was no other car, no sign of anything, and the gates were closed. There was no way it could have been a normal person who could have got through those gates at that particular time . . .'

Appendix B

Miscellaneous Information about Banshees, Death Warnings, and Apparitions

1. *The Warrenpoint apparitions*
'I was driving home with a couple of friends, just chatting and carrying on in the car. It was quite late, well after midnight, and very dark on the road. As we were passing Narrow Water wood the headlights of the car caught someone at the side of the road. I realised it was a soldier and he stepped out and flagged the car down. It was really weird, as I couldn't make out if he had anyone with him. I rolled down the window and he asked me for my driving licence. I waited a few moments and then he dropped it on the ground. I went to say something to him and he disappeared—just vanished into thin air. We couldn't believe it. We were all so stunned we didn't know what to do. Through sheer terror, I stuck my foot on the accelerator and didn't stop until I got home ...' (*Sunday News*, 30 March 1980.)

2. *Report of possible banshee and of a death warning*
(Witness was about 10 years old and living in Co Westmeath.)
'I suddenly heard an extraordinary frightening, sharp, shrill outcry. It really sounded supernatural, and I can well remember that I was filled with a violent fear ... Some two years later I had the experience of the sound of a large glass picture-frame falling on the stone-flagged floor of my grandmother's house. Three days later my grandmother's son was killed in an accident in a hayfield ...' (Mr Derek Campbell, Dalkey, Co Dublin, August 1983.)

3. *Another report of a death warning*
'When I was 10 years old my daddy became ill. On the Sunday, sitting around the fire [were] my 4-year-old brother, my 12-year-old sister, and myself. Suddenly there was a crash,

and the holy picture above the fireplace had fallen and shattered . . . Daddy died the following night. My sister was sent
to tell Daddy's sisters of his death. One opened the door and
said, "Is Patrick dead? He died at half past eleven last night"
. . . They said that they had heard the knocking and then the
banshee.' Another instance some years later: 'I went one
Sunday to visit my mother and there was a crash and the holy
picture had fallen and shattered. Mother cried and said that
one of her family had died . . . The next morning she had a
cable from America to say that her sister had died on the previous afternoon . . .' On her mother's death: 'In 1980 in the
early hours of a Friday morning I was awakened by this terrible knocking on the door. I went down but there was no-
one there, and then I knew that my mother had died about
3.30 a.m. . . .' (Mrs Ursula Hughes, Belfast.)

4. *Report of an apparition seen in Lisburn College of Further
Education*
'During November or early December of 1982 I had finished
a class in C24 [in the old attics of the building] at 4.57 p.m.
On locking the door I noticed, standing in the fire-escape
entrance, perhaps some twenty feet from the entrance to C24,
the figure of a middle-aged gentleman, about 5 foot 10 inches
tall and of fairly heavy build. He wore a dark suit of early
Edwardian style. I believe this figure to be that of the late
William Barbour, as I have seen many pictures of him. I saw
the figure for about ten seconds . . .' (Mr Bill Whitely, lecturer,
Lisburn, 1983.)

Appendix C

Bibliography

Byrne, Patrick, *The Second Book of Irish Ghost Stories*, Mercier Press, Cork, 1971.

Croker, T. Crofton, *Fairy Legends and Traditions of the South of Ireland*, 1825.

Danaher, Kevin, *Folktales of the Irish Countryside*, Mercier Press, Cork, 1967.

Dunne, John D., *Haunted Ireland*, Appletree Press, Belfast, 1977.

Feversham, Countess of, *Strange Stories of the Chase*, Geoffrey Bliss.

Foster, Jean Cooper, *Ulster Folklore*, H.R. Carter, 1951.

Greene, W.J., *A Concise History of Lisburn*, Belfast, 1906.

Gregory, Lady Augusta, *Visions and Beliefs in the West of Ireland*, volumes 1 and 2, G.P. Putnam, New York, 1920.

Gurney, Edward, *Phantasms of the Living*, 1886.

Lenox-Conyngham, Mina, *An Old Ulster House*, Dundalgan Press, Dundalk, 1946.

Leslie, Sir Shane, *Shane Leslie's Ghost Book*, Hollis and Carter, 1955.

Logan, Patrick, *The Old Gods*, Appletree Press, Belfast, 1981.

Myers, F.W., *Human Personality and Survival of Bodily Death*, Logmans Green, London, 1903.

Ó Súilleabháin, Seán, *Nósanna agus Piseoga na nGael*, Three Candles, Dublin.

Rhine, J.B., *Extra Sensory Perception*, Humphries, Boston, 1939.

Seymour, St John, *Irish Witchcraft and Demonology*, 1913.

Spence, E. O'Donnell, *The Banshee*, Sands and Co.

Spencer, Lewis, *Magic Arts in Celtic Britain*, Aquarian Press, Wellingborough, 1970.

St. Clair, Sheila, *Folklore of the Ulster People*, Mercier Press, Cork, 1971.

BIBLIOGRAPHY

St. Clair, Sheila, *Psychic Phenomena in Ireland*, Mercier Press,
Cork, 1972.

Wilde, Lady Jane Francesca, *Ancient Legends, Mystic Charms
and Superstitions of Ireland*, Chatto and Windus, London,
1925.

Index

INDEX